A PICTORIAL HISTORY OF
Marble Falls
The Land Embracing the Falls on the Colorado

Published by
The Highlander

The first vacation I remember as a child brought my family from West Texas to Lake Buchanan. It was years later that Noah Smithwick brought me down the road to Marble Falls. As a collector of books about the Texas frontier, I came across a first-edition of *Evolution of a State* and Smithwick's lively account of pioneer life – much of it centered on his experiences in the Marble Falls area – became a favorite.

Later, in visits to buy Texas longhorns for our ranch, the town and its surroundings became a favorite as well. So when Ellen and I moved here and returned *The Highlander* to local ownership with the acquisition of its sister papers in Burnet, Kingsland and Llano early in 2006, we were keenly aware of their heritage and truly appreciated this "Most Texas of Places" and its rich history.

We were honored when The Falls on the Colorado Museum asked permission to reprint this excellent book Billy Becker edited years ago for *The Highlander* and we are pleased to donate any profits from its publication to this most worthwhile organization. We encourage you to join the Museum and its directors in preserving the history of our people.

As Marble Falls' oldest newspaper, *The Highlander* has recorded the history of our community week after week for nearly 50 years. We pledge to continue to earn your trust as we chronicle our story into the new century and we hope, as with this book, you'll enjoy pausing with us from time to time to reflect on those who made this special place in Texas.

Roy E. Bode
Editor & Publisher
The Highlander
Marble Falls, Texas
September 27, 2006

Dedication and Acknowledgments

This volume is dedicated to Madolyn Frasier.

Madolyn's lifelong work to preserve and protect the history of this area was a primary element in the creation of this volume. She was one of the driving forces behind the publication of *The Valley between the Colorado and the Pedernales*, by Mary Albers Thompson and Ms. Frasier, which collected history and photos of the communities southwest of Marble Falls.

Every community should have someone so dedicated to the preservation of its lives, history, and culture. Two of her continuing goals are to produce a history of the southern part of Burnet County, an area with its epicenter in Marble Falls but stretching into Blanco and Llano Counties, and a museum to preserve and present this history and its artifacts.

This volume is another step toward those community goals. Its production has been made so much richer by her knowledge, participation and invaluable advice.

~~~~

I am indebted to *The Highlander* and publisher Sean French for allowing me a free hand in assembling the people and the photographs to make this book possible. In producing this visual history and the earlier special centennial issue, *100 Pages of Marble Falls History: 1887-1987*, *The Highlander* has provided an invaluable public service to this community.

Others have also played pivotal roles in creating this edition. Gilbert H. Jacoby worked tirelessly to help order the flood of some 800 photos and to keep the selection process manageable. Richard Stone, editor of *The Highlander*, lent his critical eye, designing ability and patience to the editing of the photographs and the final design of this book. Dennis Phillips provided technical support for scanning photos.

Betty O'Connor allowed me to select photos from the priceless collection of Elizabeth Reed Alexander which, in itself, contains much of the early history of the town. Diana Collins of the Marble Falls Library brought the other great collection of local historical images to our office and allowed us to scan them directly. Without these two collections, compiling the early visual history of the area would not be possible. Those images are irreplaceable treasures beyond value.

Other photos came from near and far, and we are indebted to all of you who contributed. This has been a community collaboration in the finest sense.

Billy Becker

© 1999, 2006 and 2021
The Highlander
PO Box 1000
Marble Falls, TX 78654

Published by: Highland Lake Publishing LP
905 3rd Street
Marble Falls, TX 78654

Introduction

May, 1999

For those who made this town their home and grew up on the banks of the Colorado and in the surrounding countryside, this pictorial history has collected these surviving images in the hope of preserving the legacy of the land and the people of the hill country surrounding the Colorado River.

The cover photo view of Marble Falls seen from the south is as breathtaking today as it was in 1899. It inspired native son Oscar Fuchs to compose "The Hills of Home."

The Colorado River valley spreads to the northwest bounded by Packsaddle Mountain and Backbone Ridge in the distance, and Thanksgiving and Slaughter Mountain nearby. Lake Marble Falls now fills most of the two miles of canyon that begins its rapid descent just above the Highway 281 bridge.

The falls no longer roar day and night, and the canyon walls no longer echo the river's noisy passage downstream. The famous fishing holes — the Trap, the Blue Hole, the Willow Hole — are long since covered and gone.

Only the Blue Bonnet Hole remains, where the Colorado has raced from the canyon and over the deep, rocky shelf for millions of years to create a half-teacup shaped depression over 100 feet deep in the sandy deposits there.

As you come down the river hill, the only immediate remnants of the visible past are the old power house, the rugged survivor of many a flood, the giant slab where the old factory building once dominated the entry to the town, now soon to be a hotel, and the almost-hidden Liberty Hall, built by founding father Gen. Adam Johnson in 1888.

Granite Mountain arises to the northwest, its eastern face the only solid semblance remaining of a giant batholithic dome rising above ground, now carved away for over a century to create the state capital, the Galveston Seawall and hundreds of other structures throughout the nation.

Lining the north side of Third Street downtown, the stone-clad walls of the Masonic Lodge building, the Turner-Evans and Badger complex, and the Ellison building still can be seen. Throughout the town you will find scattered buildings and homes from that early era, but all too many have vanished.

When the locals speak with reverence of that magnificent natural wonder, the marble falls, they are also remembering a time at this place when life was both harder and, yet, more pleasant and relaxed. Meeting on the river on a hot summer day was an almost timeless experience shared by all. It was a democratic domain that welcomed everyone, a connection to the liquid lifeblood that flowed through this land producing sustenance, pleasure and awe. No artificially-created entertainment will ever replace such emotional bonds forged on the namesake of this town. Within a couple of generations no one will remain who saw the natural falls in all its majesty and grace.

Today this area exists in social juxtaposition like the rugged, exposed granite over two billion years old and the later deposited limestone from ancient seas several million years ago, newcomers and old primal stock enfolded together to face the dramatic elements of Texas weather and the ceaseless erosion of time. Decimate or elevate, the river eventually carries both downstream to become sand on the beaches.

To this day, the river is the metaphorical process of our lives through drought and flood, whether raging beyond control or peacefully reflecting the pristine beauty of this country in the dusk of early morning. We are bound to this river just as this river is bound to this land, and we all pay homage in our hearts to the role it has played throughout our lives.

Those who come later may never know our relationship with the natural river. In creating the present lake, we have sought to control the Colorado and its damaging fury, but in doing so, we have also vanquished certain elements of its nature which made it so wonderful. One day, perhaps, the river will free itself and the falls will roar once more through the marbled canyon walls.

A Pictorial History of the Highland Lakes Area

Early Town

Looking downstream across the natural lake from near Panther Hollow at the turn of the century, very little of Marble Falls could be seen except for the cluster of buildings on Main Street and the factory building. *Photo from Elizabeth Alexander Collection, courtesy Betty O'Connor.*

The falls had attracted attention since the first Spanish explorers penetrated Central Texas and noted it on their maps as the 'Great Falls,' then as the 'Falls on the Colorado.' This is what inspired Adam Rankin Johnson to create a town on the banks of the river. By 1907, the original power and light building (foreground) had been rebuilt with stone to protect it from floods. *Photo from Elizabeth Alexander Collection, courtesy Betty O'Connor.*

While surveying state school land in 1854, 24-year-old Adam Rankin Johnson first laid eyes on the Falls on the Colorado. After the Civil War, he returned as a general, but blind from a gunshot wound. Nonetheless, he pursued his dream of a town at the Falls on the Colorado. On July 6, 1887, the charter of the Texas Mining and Improvement Company was filed in Burnet County. Ten men who came to be known as the founders of Marble Falls were the owners of the development company: Adam R. Johnson, T.E. Hammond, R.E. Johnson, W.H. Badger, C.T. Dalton, W.H. Roper, George Christian, F.H. Holloway, B. Badger and Adam Rankin. At 10 a.m. on Tuesday, July 12, 1887, lots were put on sale. Some $30,000 worth of lots ranging in price from $75 to $750 were sold. Even though two other men had tried founding a city at this same site with the same name, Gen. Johnson, TM and I completed the dream. Information from *Daily Texas Nutshell* of Bertram. *Photo courtesy Madolyn Frasier.*

Gen. A. R. Johnson built Liberty Hall 1888. Shown in this photo are: (standing) Roberta Williams, Julia Williams and Gen. Johnson. Sitting on the steps are "Miss Lou" Johnson and R. E. (Bob) Johnson. Bill and Eunice Wall bought the home in 1946. Today the restored home, filled with a fine collection of family and other historical photos, serves as a bed-and-breakfast as well as the residence of Wilburn Wall. *Photo from Marble Falls Library Collection.*

This 1908 photo from the south bank of the Colorado River shows a growing Marble Falls and the bridge built in 1891. *Photo from Elizabeth Alexander Collection, courtesy Betty O'Connor.*

In 1881, George Lacy, Dr. W.H. Westfall and N.L. Norton donated granite from the 60-acre batholithic dome on the western edge of Marble Falls to the state of Texas for the construction of a new state capitol. The men hoped the state would construct a railroad to the area to transport the material. As cattlemen, with the Mezgers and nearby ranchers, the group had driven their cows to market up north as far as Kansas. The state was building a railroad from Austin to Abilene, and added a spur to Burnet in 1882 and to Granite Mountain in 1885. In the interim, labor, often convict labor, worked to mine the granite. Ox-drawn wagons transported the stone to Burnet for final shaping prior to the construction of the spur to Granite Mountain. Between 1885 and 1887 some 15,700 loads of granite were transported to Austin. The capitol building was dedicated on May 16, 1888. *Photo from Elizabeth Alexander Collection, courtesy Betty O'Connor.*

Badger House, built in 1888 by Captain Brandt Badger (b. 1839, d. 1920), stands majestically on an entire block. Badger was a Confederate veteran who moved to Burnet from Gonzales in 1885. He moved to Marble Falls in 1887 and helped found the city. Badger built the house from Granite Mountain quarry rubble. The Badger family lived there until 1943. The house has eight rooms and six fireplaces. The home at 404 Avenue M received a Texas Historical Landmark plaque in 1974, when it was restored by the Pinson family. *Photo from Elizabeth Alexander Collection, courtesy Betty O'Connor.*

The Otto Ebeling home was built in 1891 at Sixth Street and Avenue F. Ebeling built the house for his wife Emille (Giesecke) and four kids. The Ebelings moved to Austin in 1917. The house was restored in 1982 by great-nephew Robert Lee Ebeling, Jr. and wife Jean, and recorded as a Texas Historic Landmark in 1983. The home reflects Eastlake styling and features distinctive bay windows with decorative stained glass borders. *Photo from Elizabeth Alexander Collection, courtesy Betty O'Connor.*

The railroad into Marble Falls was completed in 1889, and passengers and freight began arriving on a regular basis. The depot was completed in 1893. This photo from April 21, 1893, shows townspeople and railroad employees at the new depot on Avenue N and South First Street. The tracks remain and are still in use by J. M. Huber, Inc., for shipping calcium carbonate products refined and packaged at the site. The depot was used until 1960. Bill Bray later donated the building to the city, and it was then moved to Hwy. 281 and Avenue H in 1977, where it now serves as the office for the Marble Falls Chamber of Commerce. *Photo courtesy of Evelyn Luckie Naumann.*

The first hotel in town was built in 1888 by George and Elizabeth Hackenhull Roper and was known as the Roper Hotel. The first floor featured a dining and reception area, kitchen and family quarters. There were 12 guest rooms on the second floor and a "sample" room was used by drummers to peddle their products. Early guests included Governor Jim Hogg, who would travel to Marble Falls by railroad. In continuous use throughout its history, the structure has been called the Central Hotel, the Francis House, has served as a personal residence as well as a restaurant. Today it has been restored as the Roper Building, by Larry and Suann Adkins. A collection of historic photos graces the lobby. *Photo from Elizabeth Alexander Collection, courtesy Betty O'Connor.*

Trumpeting 'Accuracy, Promptness & Dispatch' with his flair for advertising, E. G. Michel stands in front of his establishment built in 1905. This store — and many of the other buildings on the west side of Main Street except for the last two near Second Street — burned in 1927. Michel had fulfilled his dream with the grand structure, but was only able to rebuild a one-story structure on the old site. A wealth of photographs would perish in the '27 fire.
Photo courtesy Marble Falls Library Collection.

Main Street began to fill out after the turn of the century, as this view south from Turner and Evans (left), midway between Third and Fourth streets, shows a line of businesses and homes all the way to the Central Christian Church.
Photo from Elizabeth Alexander Collection, courtesy Betty O'Connor.

Wagons loaded with cotton bales, one of the important crops of the time, sit in the middle of Main Street around 1910. *Photo from Elizabeth Alexander Collection, courtesy Betty O'Connor.*

Cotton bales are weighed at the local scales, then shipped via the railroad to nearby mills. The original factory building was intended to be a cotton mill, but after construction it was discovered that the basement was too small to house the necessary equipment. Local cotton farmers had to ship their baled cotton out of town. *Photo from Elizabeth Alexander Collection, courtesy Betty O'Connor.*

Turner and Evans Hardware and B. Badger and Sons grocery occupied the whole corner of Third and Main after the turn of the century. Later, these buildings became Huntley-Marrs department store, then J. F. & W. F. Barnes Lumber Company, which remodeled the buildings in 1946-47 in an art deco style. Barnes was followed by Foxworth-Galbraith, and now, Aunt Bee's Candle Factory. Owners Toby and Vicky McWilliams have returned the interior to its turn-of-the-century style, doctored the giant oak just north of the buildings to make it a shady-giving centerpiece of a soon-to-be outdoor market and community gathering area. *Photo courtesy Marble Falls Library Collection.*

The granite structure of Malcolm H. Reed and Co., which later became known as the Chollett building, sat on the southeast corner of Third and Main, seen here in the early 1900s. In the 1950s, large pecan and sycamore trees behind the building offered shade and served as a community gathering place when everybody came to town on Saturday. The site is now a parking lot occupied by a lone sycamore tree. *Photo from Elizabeth Alexander Collection, courtesy Betty O'Connor.*

Dr. J. R. Yett stands in front of Citizens State Bank (now site of the Marble theatre). Dr. Yett's office was on the side of the building. Behind the bank was the Bredt Hotel, now known as the fully restored Wallace House. *Photo from Elizabeth Alexander Collection, courtesy Betty O'Connor.*

Chartered in 1891, the First National Bank building on the northwest corner of Second and Main still stands. Shown (L-R) are R.H. Evans, Dr. Reed Yett and Herbert Tate. This bank was robbed of $2,875 in October, 1915, and bookkeeper Robert Heinatz was killed in the heist, which drew national attention. The two culprits were finally arrested in Snyder. This building later housed Home State Bank and City Hall; now it is the Riverbend Art Gallery. *Photo from Elizabeth Alexander Collection, courtesy Betty O'Connor.*

W.H. Andrews' implement company included one of the necessities of civilization — coffins. Located next to the Marble Falls Mercantile in the Ellison building, the area is now a continuous row of businesses, including Billy Joe DeSpain's Barber Shop and Marble Falls Glass and Mirror. *Photo courtesy the Marble Falls Library Collection.*

H.T. Ellison stands before the Marble Falls Mercantile Company on the northwest corner of Main and Third Street. Filtered gasoline was available as well as water. Ellison moved to Marble Falls in 1894 and lived in a house where the County Annex now sits at Avenue H. The spring just south of the building still exists and was a steady source of water for the household. For the first three nights the family lived there, they couldn't sleep because the falls were so loud. Then, on Saturday night the cowboys would come around, riding their horses and raising a ruckus. Ellison strung up a clothesline just higher than a horse's back in the unlit yard in preparation for the next Saturday night. The scheme proved successful, and the cowboys didn't come round anymore. *Photo courtesy Ona Lou Roper.*

The cornerstone on the Masonic Lodge building at the corner of Hwy. 281 and Third Street was set in November, 1909. The lower floor of the building served as a home for the Lois Anderson Memorial Library as well as *The Marble Falls Messenger* in the 1950s. No longer a lodge building, it now houses financial businesses. *Photo courtesy the Marble Falls Library Collection.*

Wood haulers gather in front of Turner-Evans and Badgers to begin the 40-mile trip to Fredericksburg. *Photo courtesy Marble Falls Library Collection.*

During the coldest snap in Texas history, the natural lake above the falls froze solid enough that Bob Jay was able to ride his horse across the lake and people could walk on it and 'skate' around. This photo was taken on February 11, 1899. The next day was the coldest in recorded Texas history, with a low of -23 occurring in Tulia. Even Galveston Bay iced over. The lake had frozen over in 1888 as well, but the only other time this has come close to occurring in modern times was during the great snowstorm in January, 1949. That storm dumped 11.5 inches of snow on the area, and the lake froze over, but the thickness of the ice was not enough to sustain people except in the shallowest places. *Photo courtesy the Marble Falls Library Collection.*

Bob Jay owned stables near First Street and Main and cut a rugged look on a horse. *Photo courtesy Marble Falls Library Collection.*

Kids play in the water on the south end of the falls in this turn-of-the-century photo. The kids are Edith Lee Burnam, Isabel Andrews, Gideon Hubbard, and Wilson Burnam; the child drinking from the lake is unknown. *Photo courtesy of Edith Burnam Hubbard.*

Kids play in the river bed below the toll house on the north end of the iron bridge. Built in 1891 as a toll bridge, citizens were never overjoyed about paying to cross the river. After much protesting, especially from the northern part of the county, Marble Falls bought the bridge in 1896 for $16,000, ceased charging tolls, and the toll house was torn down. *Photo courtesy of Edith Burnam Hubbard.*

Children fishing below the power house, at this time a stone, one-story sturcture, were captured in a photo taken by Annette Burnam on September 28, 1907. The kids are: Vince, Isabel Andrews, Louise Andrews and Jessie Burnam Mezger. *Photo courtesy of Edith Burnam Hubbard.*

Central Christian Church at First and Main St. was constructed in 1893, with much of the veneer from local granite. The building was later sold and became the Assembly of God Church. Recently, this building was torn down and a new Assembly of God Church constructed on the site. *Photo from Elizabeth Alexander Collection, courtesy Betty O'Connor.*

St. Frederick's Baptist Church was organized in 1893 in the home of Mrs. Dicie Yett Johnson (seated). Between 1893 and 1899, the church and school was held in the bottom of the Blazing Star Lodge building, then located near the corner of Main and Sixth Street. In 1899 the congregation moved to the "Church in the Hollow" near the railroad depot at South First Street and Avenue L. The church was rebuilt at Avenue N and First Street in 1955 and remained there until 1978, when St. Frederick's was built at its present site of Third Street and Avenue N. *Photo courtesy of St. Frederick's Baptist Church.*

Organized in 1893, the first Methodist church faced Main Street. This second structure was built in 1914 and faced East at Fifth Street and Hwy. 281. It was torn down to make way for Marble Falls National Bank and a new church was built on Bluebonnet Drive. This new building was heavily damaged by fire in 1997 and was once again rebuilt.

The First Baptist Church also went through an ordeal by fire. Organized in 1893, this wooden structure at Fifth and Main was later given a rock veneer and further remodeled. However, it burned on March 1, 1962. After 70 years in one spot, there was concern about moving the church to a new location. With an eye to the future, the church moved to its present location at Avenue E and 10th street; a second larger chapel was added as the membership rose under the guidance of Bro. Max Copeland.

A Pictorial History of the Highland Lakes Area

Early Town Scenes

Looking west down Seventh Street from a spot just east of Avenue E. *Photo courtesy of Marble Falls Library Collection.*

This home was built by George Christian in 1892. He married Juliette Johnson, daughter of Adam R. Johnson. It is a fine late Victorian, Queen Anne style structure with portruding bay windows. It later became known as the Matern home when the family of Ivo B. and Mena Matern lived there from 1908-1959. Caryl Calsyn bought the home in 1992 and restored it, receiving a Texas Historical designation in 1996. *Photo courtesy of Caryl Calsyn.*

Bottom left: M.H. Reed built this home at 416 Main just after the turn of the century. He also built the four homes on the west side of Main Street across from the Marble Falls Library just before the turn of the century, the granite building once on the southeast corner of Third and Main and his personal residence once on the southwest corner of Seventh and Hwy. 281. Mrs. J.C. 'Mammy' Reed and her family moved into this house in 1915. Reed gave the home to Mammy, his sister-in-law, who passed it on to her daughter Elizabeth, who would later give the home to Betty O'Connor. Today it is an antique store. The home has never been sold. Elizabeth graduated from Marble Falls HS in 1911 and would marry Emmitt Alexander. She compiled the photos that make up the collection that carries her name at this home. *Photo courtesy of Betty O'Connor and the Elizabeth Alexander Collection.*

Prior to the construction of the bridge in 1891 and for some time thereafter, a ferry and excursion boat would carry people across the natural lake. The boat is docking near the site of what became the Boy Scout Troop #284 encampment and is now Lakeside Park. Floods washed away the pecan trees that shaded the favorite swimming hole. *Photo courtesy the Marble Falls Library Collection.*

Sulphur and iron springs entered the Colorado just downstream from the bridge on the south side of the river. They are now covered by Lake Marble Falls. *Photo from Elizabeth Alexander Collection, courtesy Betty O'Connor.*

The John Lacy home. *Photo courtesy of the Marble Falls Library Collection.*

A group traveling on an excursion by train from Ft. Worth stops before Marble Falls Academy in 1899. Jack Blanton's grandfather, Andrew Jackson, was part of this group. The bell tower of the building was blown away in a storm. In the rear are dormatories where kids from outlying areas would live when school was in session. Known locally as the Granite School, this became the center of the Marble Falls School District when it was formed in 1908. A new high school building was added just to the west in 1938, and an elementary building was constructed just to the east in the early Fifties. Today it serves as the administration building for MFISD. *Photo courtesy of Madolyn Frasier.*

Four young men on Main Street Marble Falls. *Photo courtesy of Lee Ussery.*

Looking north on Main Street, Marble Falls, January 24, 1915. *Photo courtesy of Doug and Joy Michel.*

Barrels are loaded onto a modified 1922 Model T in a photo from 1923 taken across the street from what is now the Wallace House on Third Street. Lonnie Wilson Shaffer holds the barrel, John Henry Shaffer brings the funnel and Nuge Maugham helps roll the barrel from the ground. *Photo courtesy of Doug and Joy Michel.*

River road near Panther Hollow, which, according to the late Henry Krumb, received its name from an incident around 1903 when a mountain lion attacked a little girl after she wandered away from her parents who were fishing at the mouth of the creek. The story could never be confirmed, but the name remains. *Photo courtesy of Joe Cude.*

The narrow river road wound its ways up the south side of the natural lake below the hill where modern RR 2147 now runs. For many, this became a lover's lane for idyllic rides and picnics on the river with a sweetheart. *Photo courtesy the Marble Falls Library Collection.*

The whereabouts and date of this Marble Falls post office is still unknown. The first Marble Falls post office was established on the south side of the river on July 25, 1884, and William W. Gaston became the first commissioned Postmaster. In 1937, *The Marble Falls Messenger* ran a series by Daisy Rowney Singleton giving the history of the post office at Marble Falls. On Sept. 21, 1886 John A. Roper succeeded PM Gaston and would move the post office across the river to near the Depot, as many businesses had sprung up in this area due to the railroad. Postmaster Firman J. Rowney moved the post office around 1900 to the hill where the city was growing fastest – that is, to Main Street. A permanent, concrete structure was built at 105 Main Street in 1910 and the Post Office remained there until the 1940s, when it was moved to the lower, rear portion of the Uptown Theatre at Third and Main. In the early 1960s, under the guidance of Postmaster Granville Hearn, a more modern building was erected at Fourth and Main, which the Highland Lakes Art Guild now owns. Still outgrowing itself, Postmaster Colleen Wynn Lewis engineered the move to the present site at Mission Hills and Highway 281. *Photo courtesy Lee Ussery.*

This barber shop was located at the present site of the Marble Falls Library and had a bird's eye view of the falls. *Photo courtesy Lee Ussery.*

John Faubion, longtime editor of the *Marble Falls Messenger*, drove this Armistice Day float in 1919. Among those in the vehicle were Hodge McCleary, Carl Marrs, John Faubion Jr. and Richard Giesecke. *Photo courtesy Marble Falls Library Collection.*

1923 Burnet County Fair Queen Lillian Hooper of Marble Falls. *Photo courtesy of the Marble Falls Library Collection.*

Period photo of the Marble Falls volunteers who composed Company K of the United States Army in infantry formation. Company K was formed before the 1898 Spanish American War and saw service in that action. A poster from that era has been saved by Nita Crawford Renick and lists the names of all the men in Company K. Unfortunately, the poster would not scale down to book size and be legible. *Photo courtesy Marble Falls Library Collection.*

Pioneers

Mary Calissa Booker Wimberly, circa 1886. *Photo courtesy of D.R. Jackson.*

Above right: Adolph Carl Matern and Mary Ellen Williams Matern were married on April 25, 1888. This photo was taken on June 10, 1888. *Photo courtesy of Bill Matern.*

Alice Duncan sits ramrod straight on her horse at the John Duncan Ranch and home near Packsaddle Mountain in the 1880s. Duncan was the great aunt of Rose Gibson Metzler. In the 1873 Indian fight on Packsaddle Mountain, the wounded men were brought to the Duncan home. *Photo courtesy Rose Gibson Metzler.*

Andrew Perry Wimberly, circa 1889. *Photo courtesy of D.R. Jackson.*

Above left: Adolph Carl Matern, circa 1888. *Photo courtesy of Bill Matern.*

Martin Yett was born in 1893, and came to Marble Falls from a Post Mountain farm that belonged to his mother's family. As a young boy he was General Johnsons "guide boy" and confidant. He married Ora Shelby and they raised seven children. Mr. Yett worked at Granite Mountain and moonlighted for the Michel's at their ranch south of the river. He was stationed at Ft. Hood during WWI and lived with his son in retirement. *Photo courtesy of St. Frederick's Baptist Church.*

The Turner family in Burnet County in the late 1800s. Pictured are, front row left to right: Rose Ellen Turner (holding daughter, Isabel), Sam Turner, Julia Inez Turner Wimberly, John Jackson Turner and Ike Turner. Middle: Minnie Turner. Back row: Bud Turner, Dee Turner, Charley Turner and Nina Turner. *Photo courtesy of D.R. Jackson.*

Townsfolk look at the cave on Granite Mountain where convicts were kept at night after their labors during the day mining granite for construction of the state capitol.
Photo courtesy Marble Falls Library Collection.

Elizabeth Reed (Alexander) visits the area near the old dam with Jim Hunnicut (left) and Mose Jarmin. *Photo from Elizabeth Alexander Collection, courtesy of Betty O'Connor.*

Above left: Sadie Singleton and Julia Turner Wimberly in the late 1800s. *Photo courtesy of D.R. Jackson.*

Herman Richter in Austin Texas, in the late 1800s. *Photo courtesy of Robyn Richter.*

A buggy drives across the old bridge. *Photo courtesy of Edith Burnam Hubbard.*

Benjamin Major Gibson, from tintype. Gibson was the great grandfather of Rose Gibson Metzler. Took part in the Indian fight on top of Round Mountain in 1868 (noted in Blanco County History). *Photo courtesy Donald Ray Jackson and Rose Gibson Metzler.*

Stage coach stop and hotel in old Bluffton, which would later be covered by the waters of Lake Buchanan. The town was moved west to its present site in Llano County at the junction of Highways 2241 and 261. When Lake Buchanan becomes extremely low, isolated remnants of the town can still be found. This last occurrred in 1984. *Photo courtesy of Lynda Hallmark Gammage.*

Joseph Atkinson family, circa 1891. Pictured are, front row, left to right: Sarah Elizabeth (Lizzie) Atkinson, Joseph Atkinson (holding Julie Mae), Sarah Elizabeth (Bird) Atkinson holding Joseph Robert Atkinson and Kate Angelina Atkinson. Back row: William Bateman Atkinson, George Newton Atkinson and Henry Franklin (Frank) Atkinson. *Photo courtesy of Esther Pogue.*

The Arnold Homestead in Old Bluffton, which was later owned by W.O. Hallmark. Pictured are: Dovie Hallmark Wardlow, Leland Hallmark, Aubrey Hallmark and Old Cuff the dog. *Photo courtesy of Lynda Hallmark Gammage.*

Local students pose before the old Granite School around 1900. *Photo courtesy of Robyn Richter.*

Bertha Hoppe, circa late 1800s. *Photo courtesy of Robyn Richter.*

Double Horn School when school was held in Chunn Store near Grid Iron Creek in 1895. Two children seated are unidentified. First row, left to right: unknown, Ola Denniston Wall, Arra Anderson Rolls, Lee Alderson Whitely, Myrtle Sims Williamson, Rhonda Sims Frasier, Hattie Haywood, unknown, unknown, unknown, unknown, Stella Holman Fowler, ? Schroeter, Jess Kinser, unknown, Miles Calder and the last two are unknown. Second row: unknown, unknown, unknown, Orville Frasier (young boy in front of him is unknown), unknown, Sam Sims, Waddie Smithart, ? Schroeter (in hat), Mona Richter Struve, Alice Yett Cox, Professor W.D. Riddell, Gertie Richter Stolle, May Yett Burnam and Pauline Richter Odiorne. Standing in the door: Jane Kinser Campbell and her mother Mrs. Kinser. *Photo courtesy of Madolyn Frasier.*

Adolph Carl Matern family at Shovel Mountain in 1895. Adolph Carl Matern holding Agnes Parthana, Helen Gertrude, Ora Kathryn and Mary Ellen. *Photo courtesy of Bill Matern.*

Spicewood School in 1898. First row, left to right: Della DeSpain, Elva Boultinghouse Harkey, ? Edna DeSpain, Earnest Kaus, Lou Boultinghouse and Bert Faubion. Second row: Nannie Jackel, Lera Wall Thompson, Gustie Kaus, Gustie Hass, Iva Fowler Griffin, Nellie Wood Wedgeworth, Willie Crane Phillips, Lena Wall, John Faubion, Albert Grelle, James Riddell, Floyd McInnis, Albert McInnis and Fritz Hass. Third row: Emma Wall Naumann, Mary Wood, Jeannie Riddell Crownover, Carl Faubion, Professor W.D. Riddell, Fritz Kaus, Austin Fowler, Paul Grelle, Willie Hass and Joe Newman. *Photo courtesy of Madolyn Frasier.*

Double Horn Singing School about 1898. First row left to right: Mr. and Mrs. Copeland and son. Second row: Garrett Campbell, ?, Albert Kinser, Walters, ?, Carson Lowery, ?, Nora Alderson Chamberlain, ?, Nora Denniston Wall, Amy Campbell, Gracie Lowery and Lillie Denniston Williamson. Third row: Alice Proffit Sims, Stella Proffitt Haywood, Ola Denniston Wall, Clara Kinser Haywood, Rhoda Sims Frasier, Arra Alderson Rolls, Myrtle Sims Williamson, Lee Alderson Whitely, Lizzie Lowery Campbell, Callie Campbell Lowery, Alma Campbell and Jane Kinser Campbell. Fourth row: Jim Alderson, Jess Kinser, Hebert Copeland, ?, Waddy Smithart, Albert Williamson, Loyd Denniston, Will Williamson, Cass Sims, Giles Lamascusor Miles Calder, Andy Campbell, Truman Campbell, Tom A. Denniston and George Lowery. *Photo courtesy of Madolyn Frasier.*

The Sims home on the Colorado River at Double Horn in 1899. Left to right: Henry Frasier, Amiel standing in front of him, Mollie Sims Frasier holding Ima, Cass Sims, Sam Sims, Scott Sims, Myrtle Sims Williamson, Rhoda Sims Frasier, Tom Bible, Nora in front of him, Florence Sims Bible (holding Ed). Seated W.E. Sims and Sarah Elizabeth Keeler Sims. Between them is a photo their of son, George M. Sims, who died in 1896. *Photo courtesy of Madolyn Frasier.*

James B. Kennedy family around the late 1800s or early 1900s, at Spicewood, Texas. Pictured are, left to right: Burnam brother, Mary Jane Long Kennedy, James B. Kennedy and Ira Lee Kennedy. *Photo courtesy of Jody Bible.*

Approaching Marble Falls from the south at the turn of the century required a noisy trip across the iron bridge, complete with advertisements and personal notations. *Photo courtesy of Robyn Richter.*

A man travels across Burnet County on a good road during the horse and buggy days. *Photo courtesy of Robyn Richter.*

The old mill on Cypress Creek gave the community of Cypress Mills its name. An enormous cypress tree in the vicinity once was the largest tree in Texas and still ranks second. *Photo courtesy Madolyn Frasier.*

George Hoppe and his children, and Fritz Fuchs and his children in the early 1900s at Cypress Mill. *Photo courtesy of Robyn Richter.*

Joshua Hollingsworth, Henry Hollingsworth and Otho Burton with their hay baler in Henry Naumann's field near Spicewood in 1900. *Photo courtesy of Madolyn Frasier.*

John Walter Hays, on horse, grandfather of John Clark, and an unidentified man run a wheat thresher in the early 1900s. *Photo courtesy of John W. Clark.*

John Walter Hays shears a sheep with a pair of hand clippers in this early 1900s photo. *Photo courtesy of John W. Clark.*

Finis Mack Samford, 1915.

Hays family portrait, early 1900s. Front row, (L-R): John Walter Hays, Ellen Jones Hays, J.H.B. Hays and Grady Hays. Second row, George Hays, Florence Hays, Jessie Hays Parker and Martha Ann Hays. Back row, Ewell Hays and Oscar Parker. *Photo courtesy of John W. Clark.*

Ida Ellison, H.T. Roper and H.T. Ellison in the early 1900s in Marble Falls. *Photo courtesy of Ona Lou Roper.*

J. Edgar Roper of M. Reed and Co. in the early 1900s. *Photo courtesy of Ona Lou Roper.*

Inside the Marble Falls Mercantile during the early 1900s. Shown are: H.T. Ellison and an unknown customer. *Photo courtesy of Ona Lou Roper.*

The William Harvey and Nancie Wallace Roper family in a photo taken prior to 1914 at Pleasant Valley. William Harvey died in 1892 and Nancie raised the family and maintained the land until her death in 1921. She is buried at Pleasant Valley Cemetery. Surrounding her are, standing: George (a cousin born in 1870), Emma (born in 1868), Sally (born 1859), Ella (born 1864) and William (born 1861 in Pleasant Valley). *Photo courtesy of Ona Lou Roper.*

Baptism on Hamilton Creek at George Lyda place near Pleasant Valley about 1928. Alta Linebarger, Marie Bible and daughters Edna Bible Clunn (in bonnet) and Oleta Bible Phinney are standing on the creek bank to the right. *Photo courtesy of Ona Lou Roper.*

Herman and Walter Richter at the Richter place on Double Horn Road. *Photo courtesy of Robyn Richter.*

Esther, Walter, Rudolph, Helen and Hugo Richter. *Photo courtesy of Robyn Richter.*

Women pose on the steps of the George Christian home around the turn of the century. At the top of the stairs to the left is Ethel Johnson Guthrie (Juliett's sister), to the right is Juliette Johnson Christian, daughter of Adam R. Johnson, who married George Christian; and to the far right is their daughter, Martha Josephine (Jo) Christian. *Photo courtesy George Christian.*

George M. & Mary Jane Vickers Stinnett, the great grandparent of Dorice Saxon Jeffries. *Photo courtesy of Dorice Saxon Jeffries.*

Frank Lewis and Florence Stinnett Lewis in the early 1900s. Florence was the sister of Alice P. Stinnett Dawson and the grandmother of Dorice Saxon Jeffries. Florence and Frank are both buried in the Smithwick cemetery. *Photo courtesy of Dorice Saxon Jeffries.*

Wesley Fowler, far left, and his family in front of the Fowler home near Spicewood. Construction began on the house in 1859, but was not completed until after the Civil War. *Photo courtesy of Lou Ann Smoot.*

Iva Fowler and Stella Holman Fowler, in their late teens and all dressed up. Picture was probably made around 1900. These two good friends became sisters-in-law.
Photo courtesy of Lou Ann Smoot.

Lizzie Everett and Annie Everett Hays, around 1900. *Photo courtesy of John W. Clark.*

Ollie Hundley was one of the founders of the First Baptist Church. *Photo courtesy of John F. (Sonny) Taylor.*

Edward Ebeling family photograph taken at the Ebeling ranch, circa early 1900s. Left to right: Edward Ebeling, baby Margie and Marie Ebeling. *Photo courtesy of Annie Dee Ebeling.*

Clover Blacksmith Shop owned by Wes Burton. *Photo courtesy of Madolyn Frasier.*

Farmers Union Meeting at the Lewis Schoolhouse between Rockvale and Spicewood in the early 1900s. Pictured are, first row, left to right: John Jones, Will Brooks, Professor R.L. Bush, Thomas B. Lewis, Stonewall Jackson, John DeSpain, Litt Brooks, Sam Lewis and unknown. Second row: Calvin Hall, Henry Hall, Henry Thomas "cripple Henry" Lewis, Meredith Holloway, Tommie Lewis, Charlie Lewis, Tom Singleton, Rob Lewis and Jimmy Lewis. Back row: Jim Meredith, John Meredith, Martin Holloway, John Holloway, unknown, unknown, Tom Denniston and Jim Singleton. *Photo courtesy of Madolyn Frasier.*

Spanish Oak School students near the Spanish Oak Falls in the Turkey Bend community on November 28, 1902. *Photo courtesy of Madolyn Frasier.*

Spanish Oak Falls below Smithwick around 1900; today this site is just off Turkey Bend Road and Hwy. 1431. *Photo courtesy of Calvin Lewis.*

Panorama from the river hill at Marble Falls at the turn of the century. *Photo courtesy of Madolyn Frasier.*

Seated, left to right: Minnie Evans Henry, Nancy Chambers Evans, Ina Evans Wallace and Ann Evans Crawford. Standing: Caroline Evans Coleman, Ellen Evans Turner, Sarah Evans Jackson, Amanda Evans Hall, Mary Ann Evans Boultinghouse and Margaret Evans Hall. Picture was taken at Turkey Bend on January 1, 1902. *Photo courtesy of Madolyn Frasier.*

Hal Anderson (left) and Lois Wilson Anderson (right) with an unknown couple at the Marble Falls depot. Lois Anderson would later found the town's first library. *Photo courtesy of Agnes Hefner.*

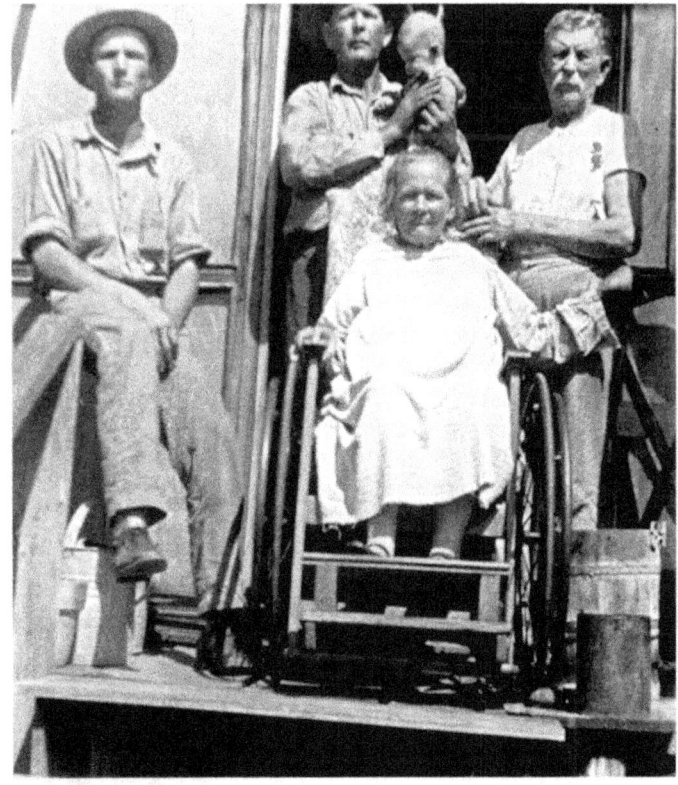

Four generations of the Ramsdell family. Left to right: J.C. Ramsdell, A.L. Ramsdell holding Myrtle Marie Ramsdell, Etta Ramsdell and E.E. Ramsdell. *Photo courtesy of Myrtle Marie Townsend.*

Matern family photo, circa 1907. Standing, left to right: Andrew Herman, Adolph Carl, Mary Ellen, Agnes Parthana and Adolph William. William Converse Skinner is sitting on horse in background.
Photo courtesy of Bill Matern.

Adolph Carl Matern family photo. Seated, Adolph Carl Matern and Mary Ellen Matern. Standing, left to right: Andrew Herman, Helen Gertrude, Agnes Parthana, William C.S., Ora Kathryn and Adolph Williams. *Photo courtesy of Bill Matern.*

Thomas A. Stinnett. He was the brother of George M. Stinnett. *Photo courtesy of Dorice Saxon Jeffries.*

Far right: H.T. Gibson, circa 1920s. *Photo courtesy of Rose Metzler.*

1909 Marble Falls junior high and high school students in front of the Granite School building. *Photo courtesy of Madolyn Frasier.*

A successful day of deer hunting in November, 1909. The driver is Arri Nobles, with Ruby Jones Miller, Casey Jones and Frank Jones in the back seat. The gun of choice seems to be the lever action .30-.30. This was Ruby Miller's first ride in a vehicle. *Photo courtesy of John E. Miller, Jr.*

Denniston family photo taken in front of the Denniston home near Double Horn Creek around 1910. Lloyd Denniston, Nolan Denniston, Frances (Franklin) Denniston, Tom Denniston, Rob Denniston and Ruth Denniston Lewis. *Photo courtesy of Madolyn Frasier.*

Dr. George Wilson attended Ohio Medical University with a degree in Dentistry. He practiced dentistry more than a year in Ohio, then he moved to Marble Falls where he practiced until he moved to San Saba in 1915. He was the uncle of Agnes Anderson Hefner. *Photo courtesy of Agnes Hefner.*

Below right: The Perry Andrew Wimberly family taken about 1910. Front row, left to right: Annis Amelia Wimberly, Mary Calissa Booker Wimberly and Perry Andrew Wimberly. Back row: Ira Andrew Wimberly and James Monroe Wimberly. *Photo courtesy of D.R. Jackson.*

Captain Alfred Ebeling, Hildegard Ebeling and Dilworth Ebeling on the jack. Elsie Ebeling and Modena Ebeling Hartzell. Picture was taken in 1912 on the Ebeling ranch. *Photo courtesy of Annie Dee Ebeling.*

Wedding photograph of Bertha Hoppe Richter and Walter Richter, taken on September 14, 1913. Pictured are, left to right: Norma Goebel, Walter Richter, Bertha Hoppe Richter, Bill Richter, unknown and Roland Hoppe. *Photo courtesy of Robyn Richter.*

Ebeling children on horse in front of the old stone house on the E.E. Ranch in Blanco County in 1913. Left to right: Ralph Max Ebeling, Elsie Gertrude Ebeling, Hildegard Anita Ebeling and Alfred Edward Ebeling. *Photo courtesy of Annie Dee Ebeling.*

Cooling their heels at the old dam in 1914 were (L-R): Grady Hays, H. B. Hays, Florence Hays and Ellen Hays, great grandparents and great uncle and aunt of John Clark. *Photo courtesy John W. Clark.*

H.T. Roper on the hood of a Buick. *Photo courtesy of Ona Lou Roper.*

Honeymoon Camp in Burnet County west of Marble Falls in the 1920s. Front row: H.T. Roper, Annie Borden, Sally Collier and Jack Collier. Back row: Gladys Roper, Addie Borden, Ida H. Ellison and Julia Collier. *Photo courtesy of Ona Lou Roper.*

Unknown man and woman standing on the framework of the Marble Falls bridge sometime before 1935. *Photo courtesy of Doug Michel.*

The original road and railroad line to Kingsland ran below Backbone Ridge. When Hwy. 1431 was constructed, it ran over the hill and the lookout with the great view of Lake LBJ and Packsaddle Mountain was created. The rail line still runs below the mountain. *Photo courtesy of Edith Burnam Hubbard.*

Spicewood Springs, now called Krause Springs, just east of 'downtown' Spicewood, where the icy cold water cascades off the cliff into the creekbed. The site has long been enjoyed as the coolest of summer refreshments. *Photo courtesy of Doug and Joy Michel.*

Believed to be one of the first cars in Marble Falls. It was purchased in Austin. Vedena Hundley Taylor (driving) chauffeurs for Helen Marrs and Zelda Beth Rubble. *Photo courtesy of John T. and Norma Taylor.*

Peanut threshing crew at Double Horn in Clarence Lewis' field in the 1940s. *Photo courtesy of Madolyn Frasier.*

Spicewood German Hall, circa 1908. First row, left to right: Otho Naumann, Max Naumann, unknown, Ernestine Naumann, Bill Naumann, unknown, unknown, unknown, Henry Bauerle, Ernest Bauerle and Carl Bauerle. Second row: unknown, unknown, unknown, Minnie Wall, Ernestine Jackel, last on right is Hattie Jackel Bauerle holding Robert. Third row: unknown, unknown, unknown, unknown, unknown, unknown, Lera Wall Thompson, Emma Wall Naumann, and last on right is Karl Bauerle holding Jacob. *Photo courtesy of Madolyn Frasier.*

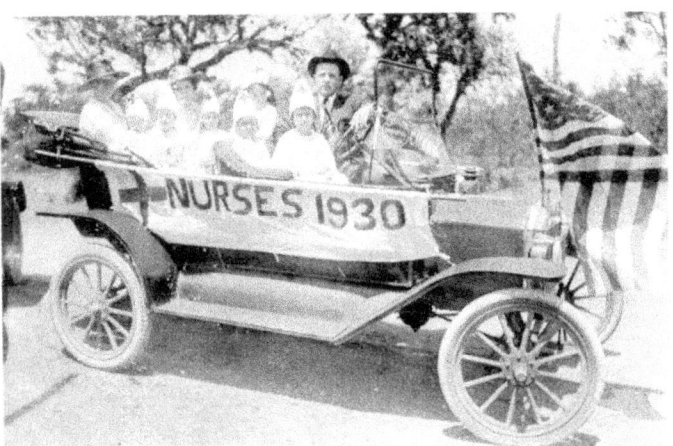

All three photos: From the photo of President Woodrow Wilson displayed on the float in the top photo, the World War I era soldier on the horse-drawn wagon, and the boys in their knee-length knickers, this parade appears to be celebration of Armistice Day, 1919, on Main Street in downtown Marble Falls. These photos, as well as the middle photo on page 25, are part of a group of similar shots from the Marble Falls Library Collection without any real date or description. However, on the next page are two photos of what appears to be the same event. One is from the Elizabeth Alexander Collection and is noted as 1919, while the other is from John E. Miller and has no date. World War I was a watershed event, ushering in the modern era while elements of the original agrarian culture would dwindle and recede over the next 50 years. *Photos courtesy the Marble Falls Library Collection.*

The parade winds south down Main Street and across Third Street past the Turner-Evans building, the Hundley-Marrs store and M.H. Reed's dry goods store. *Photo courtesy John E. Miller, Jr.*

Brothers Bub (left) and Harry Hale, who was killed in action in World War I. Bub came to own a fishing camp on the river at Pleasant Valley called Bub's Place. *Photo courtesy of John W. Clark.*

Armistice Day Parade, 1919. *Photo from Elizabeth Alexander Collection, courtesy Betty O'Connor.*

Ophelia "Birdie" Crosby Harwood horseback on Main Street at the time she was elected mayor in 1917, the first woman elected to that office in Texas, and one of the first in the nation to precede the aquisition of the vote by women. She was a popular public figure in whose term many improvements and modernizations to the town were accomplished. Below, she is shown with her husband, Dr. George Harwood, later in the 1920s. Dr. Harwood was the classic country doctor, willing to go anywhere, anytime, to serve his patients. *Photo at left courtesy the Marble Falls Library Collection, bottom photo courtesy Madolyn Frasier.*

1920s

Marble Falls Class of 1921 at their graduation: (L-R) girls, Mabel Roper Wright, Julia Hester, Ruby Jones Miller, Blanche Farquahar Dodgen, Lola Wedekind, Elizabeth Bates and Addie Samford Crawford; boys, Herbert Faubion, Norman Tate, Carl Matern, Dooley Galloway, Milton McGee and Wendal Lee Phillips. *Photo courtesy of Nita Crawford Renick.*

With her foot on the running board, this good looking young lady strikes a classic pose in this 1920s scene. *Photo courtesy of Doug and Joy Michel.*

Ladies smoking wasn't fashionable in the 20s and 30s, but this young woman flaunts the times by slipping down to the river for a cigarette. *Photo courtesy of Doug and Joy Michel.*

Ora Dorothy Dawson Saxon (on left), mother of Dorice Saxon Jeffries of Austin. *Photo courtesy of Dorice Saxon Jeffries.*

Below left: Myrtle Elvin Taylor, H.T. Roper and Virginia Beth Taylor, circa 1924. *Photo courtesy of Ona Lou Roper.*

Opal Kennedy Birch and Ruth Lusinger below the old mill in the 1920s. *Photo courtesy of Jody Bible.*

Jack Luckie (left) and Jim Luckie (third from left) relax with friends by a Model T. With the coming of Henry Ford's Model T in 1909, the mobility of the nation changed. With heavy thunderstorms ruthlessly washing out roads in the rocky hill country, travel was tough to manage with wagons and horses. With the coming of vehicles, public demand for better roads and bridges increased. *Photo courtesy of Evelyn Luckie Naumann.*

With increased mobility, Marble Falls adapted to the times by promoting fishing and hunting. This pitch to tourism began with the railroad in the 1890s, would increase with the advent of cars and trucks, and continues to fuel the area's businesses. With great scenery, wildlife, and, of course, the river and the impounded lakes – Buchanan, Inks, LBJ, Marble Falls and Travis – the Highland Lakes have become a retirement haven and vacation playland with a fast-growing population. *Photo courtesy of John T. (Sonny) Taylor.*

The Unknown Photo. Sometimes a good cigar can be more than a good smoke. Bravery comes in many forms, and so does humor. Whatever is really going on in this early photo (sometime in the '20s) probably will never be known, for it was never picked up at Michel's by the person who dropped off the film. However, the content is so amusing that it has been kept around for more than 75 years. *Photo courtesy of Doug and Joy Michel.*

Helene Matern Kellesberger, Winifred Kellesberger Vass and Edna Bosche enjoy the sun on the riverbed below the Marble Falls bridge near Ed and Helen Giesecke's home in 1920. *Photo courtesy of Ed Giesecke.*

Marie Ebeling and Rubin Houy in the 1920s. The couple would later wed. Marie became librarian for the Lois Anderson Memorial Library in the 1950s. *Photo courtesy of Annie Dee Ebeling.*

Doctoring cattle on the EE Ranch in the 1920s. Pictured are, left to right: Pancho, Papa Max Ebeling, a standing visitor, Fred Hall and Ralph Ebeling. *Photo courtesy of Annie Dee Ebeling.*

Sawing wood on the Ebeling ranch in the 1920s. Pictured are, left to right: Max, Alfred and Ralph Ebeling. *Photo courtesy of Annie Dee Ebeling.*

Below right: Papa Max Ebeling, Hildegard and Alfred going to school in Austin, during the 1920s. *Photo courtesy of Annie Dee Ebeling*

Snowfall covers old bridge in early 1930s. *Photo courtesy of John E. Miller, Jr.*

Ira Lee and Flora Kennedy in the early 1900s in Marble Falls. *Photo courtesy of Jody Bible.*

Frank and Cenia (Ricketson) Gunn on their golden wedding anniversary, July 4, 1951. *Photo courtesy of LaRhesa Gunn McNair.*

In April 1912 the Bruns family came to Marble Falls from Varel, Germany. Karl Emil Heinrich (Henry) Bruns with his wife Anna Helene (Helen) Margarete Engelbert Bruns brought their eight children Antonie, John, Henry, Anton, Helen, August, Martin and Fritz. Two more children Alfred and T.C. were born in Texas in Fayette County. They stayed with Henry's sister Antonie Marie (Bruns) Krumm and her husband Carl Krumm. They then moved to Fayette County where Helen's uncle and aunt, Anton and Anna Bunjas lived. In 1920 they moved back to the Marble Falls area. Shown at a family picnic in the 1920s are, front row, left to right: T.C., Helen, Henry and Alfred. Back row: Martin, Toni, Anton, Henry, John, August, Helen and Fritz. *Photo courtesy of Viola Bruns.*

The Rockvale Methodist Church between Double Horn and Spicewood is shown around 1904. Only the cemetery now remains. When the church was torn down, the stone was used as the veneer on the Methodist parsonage at Sixth Street and Avenue G. *Photo courtesy of Lou Ann Smoot.*

Rockvale Camp meeting in the 1920s. Rockvale lies between Double Horn and Spicewood, with the cemetery still present on the north side of the county road. *Photo courtesy of Madolyn Frasier.*

1928 Smithwick High School students. First row, left to right: Stillman Hood, Layton Cox, Lindsey Lewis, Lowell Hall, Lofton Meredith and Malcolm Heffington. Second row: Clarice Hall Pafford, Myrl Gibson Heine, Ruby Lewis Bolm, Thelma Hood Fox, Elsie Meredith Heffington, Phillip Lewis, Ernest Phillips and Pearl Pafford Duncan. Third row: Ida Mae Hood Mobley, Margie Gibson, Nora Pafford Kincheloe, Teacher Truitt Mobley, Estaline Hall Doyle, Myrtice Hall Turner and Pauline Gibson Ricketson. *Photo courtesy of Madolyn Frasier.*

Honeymoon Camp, owned and still operated by Robert Mezger and his family, was a favorite camp ground with great fishing on the granite shoals on the Colorado River. Shown at the river's edge in this 1920s photo are: in the front are H.T. Roper and Gladys Roper; in back are Ben Collier, Julia Collier, H.T. Ellison, Ida Ellison, Addie Borden, Jim Borden, Ed Roper, Jack Collier, Annie Borden and Roy Borden. *Photo courtesy of Ona Lou Roper*

Back in camp are (L-R): Gladys Roper, Addie Borden, Ben Collier and Jimmy Roper. *Photo courtesy of Ona Lou Roper.*

80th birthday of Mrs. N.C. Samford in 1937. Seated in front are Fine Hardin and Mrs. Boozer. Standing are: Mrs. W.D. Stuart, Mrs. Daugherty, Mrs. A.C. Fote, Mrs. Riddell, Mrs. McClure, Mrs. Samford, Mrs. McMillan, Mrs. Jay, Mrs. Parker, Mrs. Holman and Mrs. Waldrop. *Photo courtesy of Nita Crawford Renick.*

Edwin and Louise Hohenberger going for a ride in their 1926 Chrysler. *Photo courtesy of Annie Harton.*

 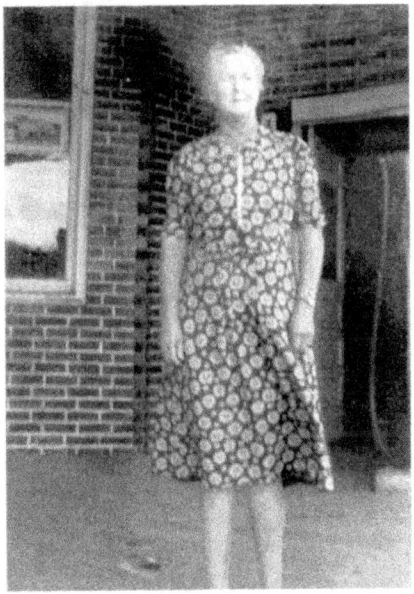

Frank Jones (left) and his wife operated a service station on the northeast corner of Main and Second Streets in the 1920s. The building was remodeled in the 1990s and has housed restaurants in recent years. *Photos courtesy of John E. Miller Jr., D.D.S.*

The Roper Hotel, taken from the corner of Third and 281. At the time of this photo it was called Central Hotel. *Photo courtesy of Doug and Joy Michel.*

E.G. Michel. *Photo courtesy of Doug and Joy Michel.*

One of the reasons Michel's was known far and wide was due to the aggressive advertising of E. G. Michel, who painted signs on all approaches to Marble Falls. According to a family story, one time E. G. was out in the country painting a Michel's sign on a rock, and the farmer who owned the land came up and objected to the sign. E. G. stopped his painting and the farmer defiantly kicked the rock over, only to find to his dismay Michel Drugs boldly painted on the bottom. *Photo courtesy of Forest F. and Midge Faubion.*

E. G. Michel, Jr., Bernetta Michel, Beth Michel and Gus Michel pose in this 1918 portrait of the children of Ernst G. and Lillie Agnes Michel. *Photo courtesy of Doug and Joy Michel.*

E. L. Michel (left) and Victor Bredt (second from left) are shown in the three-story Michel's Drug Store before it burned in 1927. *Photo courtesy of Doug and Joy Michel.*

The west side of Main Street as it appeared before the 1927 fire. *Photo courtesy of Doug and Joy Michel.*

The fountain at Michel's Drug Store has always drawn a crowd. *Photo courtesy of Doug and Joy Michel.*

The early morning revealed the devastation of the 1927 fire, with smoke still rising from the smouldering rubble. Only the last two buildings on the southern end of the block escaped the flames. *Photo courtesy of Doug and Joy Michel.*

Only the rock veneer of stores remain following the devastating fire of 1927. *Photo courtesy of Doug and Joy Michel.*

Ernst Gustav Michel stands in front of Michel's in 1930, as the drug store took on its final configuration following the 1927 fire. *Photo courtesy of Doug and Joy Michel.*

Both photos: Almon Kirchhoff views the tornado damage on the Rudolf Ebeling ranch some three miles south of town in April, 1927. A tornado would take off the roof of the old mill on August 5, 1930. A twister would skip over Granite Mountain in the great 1957 cloudburst which would drop 13 inches of rain in less than four hours and trigger powerful floods. Another would brush through Channel Oaks and the Charlie Taylor Ranch in the early 1960s. But the greatest damage would happen on Friday, May 13, 1995, when a tornado would cut a swath from Horseshoe Bay through the southwestern and northern parts of Marble Falls and the Hamilton Creek area. This tornado would never really set down hard, luckily would skip over three schools filled with children, and did not cause any fatalities. However, the extensive damage from the wind and hail would make it the costliest storm in Marble Falls history. *Photos courtesy of Annie Harton.*

Jean and Jane Taylor, circa 1928. *Photo courtesy of Sonny Taylor.*

The Toggery on Main Street in the 1920s which later burned in the 1927 fire. Employee John Miller is shown second from left, while Emmett Fowler is second from the right. The Highlander later occupied this spot on Main Street until the paper moved south of the river to Gateway Park in 1997. *Photo courtesy of John E. Miller, Jr.*

The great flood in the summer of 1899 washed away the wooden power house, according to the June 15th edition of the *Marble Falls Messenger*. Gen. Adam Johnson, who had been looking for investors in the town, immediately had the power house rebuilt with stone. As the town and the need for greater power grew, the powerhouse was modified to accommodate new and larger generators. The level of the natural lake was raised with a concrete dam some five feet high and a new intake for the power house (middle photo) was built. The powerhouse itself was remodeled, with a side opened up to bring in the new generators (bottom left), holes cut in the floor to install them; then an offset was rebuilt and a second, open story was framed up (bottom right) and a new roof was added. By the 1930s the powerhouse had assumed its final form that we still see today. Except for a short portion that survived on the south side of the falls, the concrete dam was blown up in a spectacular explosion on July 30, 1951, which marked the completion of Max Starcke Dam and the filling of Lake Marble Falls. With that, the powerhouse became a relic, a century-old survivor from the old town. *Top photo courtesy of Marble Falls Library Collection. Bottom photos courtesy of John W. Clark.*

1930s

E.E. Ramsdell poses for a snap shot on October 9, 1930. He was the father of Charles Ramsdell, John Creary Ramsdell, Frank Ramsdell, William Beecher Ramsdell, Eugene C. Ramsdell and Kathleen Ramsdell O'Hair. *Photo courtesy of Myrtle Townsend.*

Percy Lusinger, Leo Gibson, Albert Lusinger and Joe Gibson go native on the old falls in 1930. *Photo courtesy of Rose Gibson Metzler.*

Far right: Hildegarde and Nookie Ebeling standing in the old dam structure at Marble Falls. *Photo courtesy of Annie Dee Ebeling.*

Ethel Wayne Penny, H.T., Leo and Ray (Bunny) Gibson and Old Blue at the Gibson homestead in 1930s. *Photo courtesy of Rose Metzer.*

Far left: Ira Lee Kennedy at vegetable and fruit stand in the 1930s. *Photo courtesy of Jody Bible.*

Frieda and John Chollett. *Photo courtesy of Eulala Chollett Stalcup.*

Willie Gibson in 1930s on the Gibson homestead. *Photo courtesy Rose Gibson Metzler.*

Estella Hohenberger Immel, left with accordion, and her brother, Hugo Hohenberger, photographed in the 1930s at the old Rudolph Ebeling place where they grew up as the children of Edwin and Louise Hohenberger. The family had their own band, with papa Edwin playing the violin, Hugo playing the saxophone and drums, Estella the accordion, and brother Alwin the piano as well as singing. They played many times at the Shovel Mountain school, Saturday night house dances and various community gatherings. *Photos courtesy of Annie L. Hohenberger Harton.*

Employees at the Certified Labs Factory in 1931. John Thompson is on the back row, fifth from the left. Florence Thompson (Hudgins) is the seventh lady, from the left, on the front row, Theresa Thompson Gass is the fifth lady, from the left on the second row, and Alice Jean Tatum is the second from the right on the second row. *Photo courtesy of Gloria Wagner.*

John Thompson was the proprietor of the bar and pool hall in 1937. It was across the street from Barnes Lumber Yard. Customers pictured are: Bill Faubion and Ed Coats. *Photo courtesy of Gloria Wagner.*

Standing left to right: William C. Skinner Matern and Mary Evelyn Matern. Seated: Mary Ellen Matern and Adolph C. Matern. *Photo courtesy of Bill Matern.*

Mary Ellen Matern holding William Matern and W.C. Matern. *Photo courtesy of Bill Matern.*

Herman LaBlack at Granite Mountain in 1932. *Photo courtesy of Myrtle Townsend.*

Workers at Granite Mountain in 1932. *Photo courtesy of Myrtle Townsend.*

Far left: Matern family gathering. Standing left to right: Mary E. Matern, Adolph C. Matern, Ulrich VarnHagan, Mina Matern and Ivo Matern. Seated: Helene Matern Kellersberger and Louise Matern Ebeling. *Photo courtesy of Bill Matern.*

Annie Dee Hyatt and Silver on the Franklin ranch in 1936. *Photo courtesy of Annie Dee Ebeling.*

This home was built by Crosby family at 105 Pecan Valley Drive, and came to be known as Marble Hall. When the Crosby family moved, it was occupied by Dr. and Mrs. George Harwood. *Photo courtesy of Agnes Hefner.*

Far left: Annabell and Gene Ussery with son, Lee Ussery in September of 1936. *Photo courtesy of Lee Ussery.*

S.H. and Mattie Ussery with grandson, Lee Ussery in September of 1936. *Photo courtesy of Lee Ussery.*

Pickers harvest peaches at the Kurt Schroeter orchard at Double Horn around 1935: (L-R) Alva Haydon, Minnie Haydon, Nellie Haydon, Haydon kids, Lena Bailey (back to camera), Mary Lou Bailey, unknown pickers, and (far right) Carl Bailey. *Photo courtesy Tommy Bailey.*

Center right and bottom right: In 1937, Marble Falls celebrated the opening of the new bridge over the Colorado, constructed after the iron bridge had been washed away in the flood of 1935. With former Mayor Birdie Harwood in the lead, the parade started from the bridge. Shown are horseback riders and the Marble Falls Fire Department's first real firetruck purchased in 1936. *Photo courtesy John E. Miller, Jr.*

Walter, far left, and Marie G. Richter, sitting in the rocker at back, gather with friends and family at the Richter house in Marble Falls. Bill is sitting on the fence mooning at Hilda, third from left; Hugo at the bottom right is feeding a young lady. What is really going on is anyone's guess, but they seem to be having fun doing it. *Photo courtesy Robyn and Walter Richter.*

Eating barbecue on the old river on March 20th, 1937, looks like it could be serious business. From the left is Fred Golding, with an unknown man peeking over his shoulder, Gordon Farned eating a rib, Jack Nagle in the hat, Harry Buck with the glasses, E.C. Alexander with a rack of ribs, and Jimmy Seaholm bending into the photo on the far right. Looks political – why else would you eat barbecue in a suit. *Photo courtesy Betty O'Connor, the Elizabeth Alexander Collection.*

1935 Fairland School picture. First row, left to right: Leona Wagner, Kathryn Ferguson and Olora Ricketson. Second row: Don Lee Wilkins, Deward Ferguson, L.D. Ferguson, Bill Nowotny and Melvin Steffey. Third row: William Matern, Mildred Nowotny, Elma Nowotny, O.J. Nowotny, Lyndon Ferguson and Gary Edwards. Back row: Leslie Peterson, Vernon Farmer, Teacher Lucille Love, Gwendolyn Latham, Lanora Wagner and Lenabelle Steffey. *Photo courtesy of Bill Matern.*

1935-1936 Double Horn School. First row, left to right: George Koch, W.C. Sims Jr., Malcolm Frasier and Kenneth Proffitt. Second row: J.E. Berry, George Sims, Edward Koch, Morris Thompson and Clifford Koch. Third row: Mary Lou Bailey Szymanski, Nita Joyce Koch Boutin, Ernestine Lewis Baker, Joe Henry Frasier, Billie Joyce Wall Hall, Bertha Mae Frasier Wagenfuhr and Theodore Koch. Fourth row: Iona Hart Becker, Lois Thomas Jackson, Betty Jo Howard Gibson, Eva Mae Fry Sims and Frank Thomas. Fifth row: Ernest Koch, Vere Howard, Edward Frasier, Teacher John Askew, Teacher Mrs. E.S. Cornelius and Hannah Engelbart Cox. *Photo courtesy of Madolyn Frasier.*

Marble Falls second graders in 1936 included, front (L-R): Mary Castenada, Maxine Shaffer, Virginia Mauldin, unknown, unknown, G. Barnes, Laverne, unknown; back row, William Herrington, Clayton Nolen, J. W. Kovone, unknown, unknown, unknown, Walter Furley, unknown, Doug Michel, Sonny Taylor. *Photo courtesy of Doug and Joy Michel.*

Far left: John Thompson holding Joyce Thompson VanDeWalle. Gloria Thompson Wagner is holding Spot the dog. Circa 1937. *Photo courtesy of Gloria Thompson Wagner.*

Arthur Ussery on a horse named Domino in front of Arthur and Winnie Ussery's house on Main Street in Marble Falls in July of 1937. *Photo courtesy of Lee Ussery.*

Social gatherings as well as boxing matches were held at the factory when Certified Labs occupied the building in the 1930s. At this social gathering around 1938, Nettie Thompson Templin is shown to the far right. *Photo courtesy of Gloria Thompson Wagner.*

Far left: Essie Kennedy Terry, circa 1938. *Photo courtesy of E.V. Terry Jr.*

Nod Terry, 18 years old, circa 1938. *Photo courtesy of E.V. Terry Jr.*

John Taylor, Sonny Taylor, Myrtle Elvin Andrews, Jane T. Wagenfuhr, Jean Stover and Vedina Taylor. *Photo courtesy of Sonny and Norma Taylor.*

Kathleen Ramsdell O'Hair, John Ramsdell, Minnie Young Ramsdell, Lorene Darter Ramsdell holding Mattie Kathleen Ramsdell and William Beecher Ramsdell. Circa 1938. *Photo courtesy of Myrtle Townsend.*

Ray Gibson riding Old Blue in 1938 on the Gibson homestead, part of which was flooded by Lake LBJ and the rest is now a part of Horseshoe Bay. *Photo courtesy Rose Gibson Metzler.*

Mr. Ramsdell standing in front of Sinclair gas station at the southeast corner of Fifth Street and Hwy. 281 around 1938. *Photo courtesy of Myrtle Townsend.*

This late 1930s photo shows the Heffington family of Smithwick: (L-R) Lynn, Lillian, Bradley, Boyd, Price, Malcom, Fred, Ruth and Gaston Heffington. *Photo courtesy Ruth Heffington Allen.*

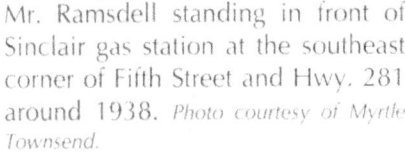

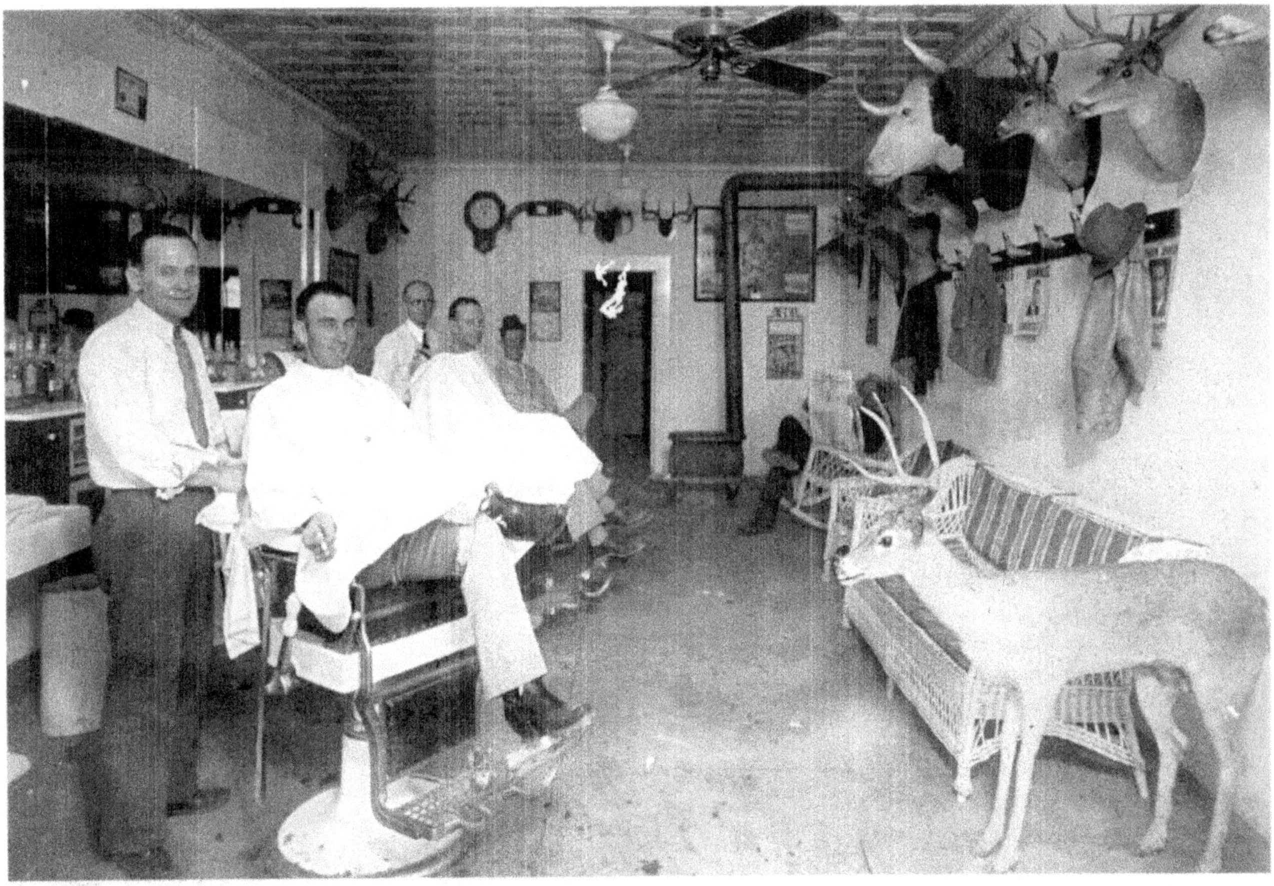

Big horns graced the interior of Walter Cox's barbershop on the west side of Main Street in the 1930s. The shop was known as the Buckhorn and survived into the 1960s with Paul Lynn cracking jokes and carrying on with the news of the day. *Photo courtesy of Anna Frances Cox Herring.*

Looking south from downtown across factory building toward the river. Circa 1930s. *Photo courtesy of Madolyn Frasier.*

Alva Haydon and Johnny Bailey drilling a water well in the 1930s. *Photo courtesy Tommy Bailey.*

E.G. Michel had the first radio in town and it became a tradition to listen to the election results there. Among those pictured are (L-R) John Taylor, Wendal Lee Phillips, Leon Nolen and, on the far right, Alfred Shifflett having a little fun on the sidewalk on Main Street in front of Michel's. *Photo courtesy of Doug and Joy Michel.*

Ralph Ebeling Sr. eyes an unrepentant Angora goat he'd roped. During time of severe drought conditions, many cattle ranchers would diversify their range stock with sheep and the hardy Angoras. In the great drought of the 1950s, Central Texas became the mohair capital of the world. *Photo courtesy of Annie Dee Ebeling.*

These kids gathered at the old roadside park on the river hill around 1940. Everyone's favorite lookout and summer gathering place was later closed by the property owner, much to the locals' dismay, in favor on a roadside stop across the highway. The 'new' roadside stop had little charm, but a good view at first; now trees and brush obstruct much of it. The historic rock pavilions of the old roadside park still exist between Kirby Eye Center and Russo's Texitally Cafe in Gateway Park. Back row: Reta Berry, Hattie Herrington, William Matern, Carlyle Wall, Jimmy Crownover, Max Haile, Lola Holland, Joyce Fry, Edith Burnam, Don Cude and Joy Green. Middle Row: Bobby Burnam, Lillian Furley, Betty Rosebond, Lee Phillips, Bula Fae Thomas, Don Berry and Cecil Nolen. Front row: Doris Elan Rambo, Agnes Rowden, Patsy Mobley, Bonnie Shirley, Olga Ruth Fluitt, Patsy Ruth Bible, unknown and Benetta Thomas. *Photo courtesy of Bill Matern.*

1940s

After WWII, Ralph (middle) and Richard Giesecke (right), assisted by John Bruns (left), opened Giesecke Brothers Supermarket on Main Street where the MF Police Station is now located. The business was so successful that the brothers opened a new store on Highway 281 at Sixth Street, now the site of Security State Bank, giving Marble Falls a modern grocery. They would later sell the store to HEB. The brothers would play a key role in the modern development of town. *Photo courtesy of Richie Giesecke.*

High school girls gather around at the entrance of the then new high school building in 1940. *Photo courtesy of Eulala Chollett Stalcup.*

Taking a field day, these 1940 school girls shyly face the camera at the old Alexander Dam on the Colorado. *Photo courtesy of Eulala Chollett Stalcup.*

Birthday party in 1945 at Crawford home at Fourth and Avenue F which included: front (L-R), Tommy Shifflett, Joe Clayton Herrington, Priscilla Hefner Stapleton, August Ray Herrington, Sharon Adams Rawson, Frances Clark, Evelyn Luckie Naumann, Gina Shifflett Ronhaar, Henrietta Herrington Lewis holding Kay Ellen Hammons Griffin; back row, Audie Herrington, Derrel Cowan, Buddy Smith, Calvin Cowan, Nita Ruth Crawford Renick, Geraldine LaForge Williamson, Viola Bruns, Wilma Gene Becker Tatum, Hilda Ruth Smith Larremore. *Photo courtesy of Nita Crawford Renick.*

The city of Marble Falls had leased some four acres to the Boy Scouts just above the falls where Lakeside Park is today. In this 1940s photo, Boy Scouts and their leaders spent time at Camp Tom Wooten near Austin. Shown are: Clayton Nolen, Harold Kennedy, Beecher Ramsdell, W. L. Atwood, Bill Souja, Doug Michel and Donald Crawford. *Photo courtesy of Doug and Joy Michel.*

Ralph Ebeling and Annie Dee Hyatt at the Walnut Church at the Walnut Creek Church on their wedding day, December 28, 1941. *Photo courtesy of Annie Dee Ebeling.*

Sarah Gibson home on the Colorado River is shown in 1942. The home sat on the Gibson homestead, the LGS Ranch, which Lake LBJ covered except for an area where Horseshoe Bay Country Club now sits. Shown in this portrait of the Gibson family are: kneeling (L-R) Bill and Roy Gibson; standing Ira, Bessie, Marie, Anna Lou, B.M. (Hoot), Esterrea, Bernice and I.V. Gibson. *Photo courtesy of Anna Lou Moore.*

Family and friends gathered with Virgil Haydon, upper right, for this photo at Double Horn when he was on leave during WWII. Back row (L-R): Brian Frasier, Carl Frasier, Lillie Frasier, Joe Frasier, Minnie Haydon, unknown, Lou Bailey, Johnny Bailey, unknown, and Virgil Haydon. Front row: unknown girl, Alva Haydon, Madolyn Frasier, Bonnie Frasier, Bertha Mae Frasier, Mary Lou Bailey, Vida Haydon and Nellie Haydon. *Photo courtesy of Tommy Bailey.*

John and Minnie Ramsdell with their children, J.C. Jr., Arthur Lee, Myrtle Oakley, Arthur Lee Jr., Myrtle Marie and the Lennox Oakley family. *Photo courtesy of Myrtle Townsend.*

Family and friends pose for an afternoon photo at the Kennedy home in Pecan Valley around 1942. *Photo courtesy of Jody Bible.*

Walter B. and Lenora McKinnerny of Cow Creek, circa 1948. Pictured are, left to right: Walter B. and Lenora McKinnerny. Children, Mary Ann, Walter L., Marjorie N. and Rosie L. *Photo courtesy of Marjorie M. Phipps.*

Myrtle Seale at the old bridge to Johnson Park, circa 1948. *Photo courtesy of Jody Bible.*

Everyone came out to play in the 11.5-inch snow in late January, 1949, the largest recorded snowfall in Marble Falls history. Temperatures fell well below zero and set official records for the area unbroken to this day (Bergstrom AFB recorded -5 degrees). Shown are: Doris, Velma and G.B. Gibson, Johnny Baily holding son Tommy, Mary Lou Bailey Szymanski and Klemons (Butch) Szymanski. *Photo courtesy of Tommy Bailey.*

Myrtle Heimann Dittmar, Estella Hohenberger Immel and Annie Kott Pressler in the spring of 1935. The old cotton mill can be seen in the background. *Photo courtesy of Annie Harton.*

Ona Lou Schulze Roper in her prom dress in 1944. *Photo courtesy of Ona Lou Roper.*

Looking northwest from the bridge, the top three levels of the falls are revealed. Today, when the lake is lowered, the bottom two levels and others down the canyon are completely covered in sand. Prior to the creation of Lake Marble Falls, floods would scour away the sand. *Photo coutesy of Eulala Chollett Stalcup.*

The River

Looking downstream (eastward) from below the bridge after a heavy snowfall. *Photo from Elizabeth Alexander Collection, courtesy Betty O'Connor.*

Midway down the canyon of the Colorado River during a rise, taken in the early 1900s. *Photo courtesy of Edith Burnam Hubbard.*

Jack Luckie at the Trap, with the lower falls and Alexander Dam in the background. *Photo courtesy of Mrs. Jack Luckie.*

This photo shows the first construction effort (shortly after 1908) to build the Alexander Dam. Three different efforts would be made, but lack of funding and the devastating effects of floods would doom the project. *Photo from Elizabeth Alexander Collection, courtesy Betty O'Connor.*

This shows the dam as the substructure was nearing completion, but a flood would wreck the project; this was as good as it would get. The river's current gathered force as the canyon made a right turn (see last photo of page 97) and the simple structure on the south side (far side) could not withstand the pressure and would be washed completely away by the raging Colorado. *Photo courtesy of Duane Michel.*

At one time, optimism ran so high that color postcards were made showing the dam under construction. Concrete structures built during the construction can still be seen today on top of the hill on the north side of the canyon. *Postcard courtesy of Ona Lou Roper.*

Both pages: This famous series of photographs shows the destruction of the iron bridge on June 14, 1935. The flood, which was the result of heavy rains upstream, had risen to some 40 feet when the structure went down and would crest at 62 feet. When the water first breeched the stone supports, virtually everyone in town gathered at each end of the bridge, uneasily eyeing the rising waters. From around 10 a.m. until the bridge finally collapsed at 3:05 p.m., people would drive over it and teenage boys would race its length on foot. Allegedly, one of the teenage Wagenfuhr boys was the last person to run across just moments before the bridge was struck by a large pecan tree, which buckled the support structure. Within minutes the river claimed the rest of the bridge. The existing Hwy. 281 bridge was completed in 1937 and is some 10 feet higher than the 1891 bridge. But, as the old timers say, there's plenty of big pecan trees upstream. *Photos courtesy of Joe Cude.*

The Ferry on the Colorado River at Marble Falls, circa 1936. The old bridge had washed out on June 14, 1935 and the new one had not been completed yet. Pictured are: unknown, Beecher Ramsdell, unknown, unknown, Rob Crownover, Odie Kreger, Kurt Schroeter, Albert Lusinger, Fred Worcester (ferry operator), Toni Krumm, Armin Matern, Eva Matern and Greta Wenmohs Schroeter. *Photo courtesy of Madolyn Frasier.*

The Colorado River was on a rampage in 1942 at the Marble Falls bridge. *Photo courtesy of Annie L. Hohenberger Harton.*

The major flood which occurred in September, 1952, became the first severe test of Max Starcke Dam. *Photo courtesy of Madolyn Frasier.*

Aerial view over Marble Falls taken March 3, 1941 by Mrs. Joe Tod showing the east side of town, Second, Third, and Fourth Streets and Avenue E, and the river from just below the bridge all the way to the Bluebonnet Hole where the Colorado River emerges from the canyon that starts at the falls. *Photo courtesy Mrs. Joe Tod.*

This second aerial view shows the bridge and the falls as well as the confluence of Backbone and Whitman Creeks. *Photo courtesy of Mrs. Joe Tod.*

The tunnel under Starcke Dam under construction in May of 1950.

1951 Wirtz Dam personnel. First, left to right: Harry Norberg, David P. (Pat) Stanford (plant machinists), P.C. Sauer (electrician), W.H. Miller (operator) and M.Q. Scott (operator). Second row: John R. Hammons (operator), John H. Ealey (operator), Frank H. Beyer Jr. (operator), George W. Newlin (operator) and supervisor C.R. Jones. Third row: Walter Colley (janitor), J.V. Jones (electrician), James R. Nolan (assisstant operator) W.G. Kuykendall (operator) and Don Bridges (operator).

On July 30, 1951, as thousands gathered from all across the area to see the blast, the retainer dam some five feet high which ran the length of the falls to channel water to the intake to the old power house was blown up using 1,000 pounds of gelignite explosives. It was the end of the marble falls as we knew them. The fishermen who loved the falls and the fishing holes cussed the event and were deeply saddened, but many cheered the beginning of a new era. *All photos courtesy of LCRA Archives.*

Calcutta poles and big cats

Hugh K. Holland shows off a big yellowcat on Main Street around 1927, enough to feed his wife Nellie and their 11 kids. *Photo courtesy of Doug and Joy Michel.*

John Taylor and Don Bridges look at a large yellowcat held by a lucky angler on Main Street in Marble Fall in front of the Reed/Cholett building. *Photo courtesy of Billy Becker.*

Judy Jackson with a large fish caught in Colorado River by her father, Vernon Jackson in 1947. *Photo courtesy of LaRhesa Gunn McNair.*

Tate Bradley, doing some serious fishing. *Photo from Elizabeth Alexander Collection, courtesy Betty O'Connor.*

Jack Luckie with hand-made Calcutta pole — the yellowcat fisherman's pole of choice — and the big yellowcat in front of Vernon Templins's garage on the west side of Hwy. 281 between Fourth and Fifth Streets. The building would later become the home of the Marble Falls Chamber of Commerce. *Photo courtesy of Opal Luckie.*

Jack Luckie, assisted by David Hartzell, holds the 72 pound yellowcat caught at the Trap in 1942. By local legend, this was the largest catfish caught by pole on the river. Sonny Taylor and Archie Barnes helped Luckie land the big cat. Yellowcats hold to the bottom when hooked and this one was strong enough to fight his way to a sanctuary. When the flathead went under a rock, Sonny and Archie used a boat to manuever the lunker away from the obstruction, carefully hand-pulling the line so Luckie could successfully land the fish. Luckie earned renown as one of the best among the local cadre of serious cat fishermen in the era before the dams were built. These same fishermen always, even those that survive to this time, bemoaned the loss of the great fishing hole which produced so many large yellowcats. *Photo courtesy of Opal Luckie.*

The Trap: the best damn fishing hole in the state, claimed local cat fishermen, and there was little to dispute the boast. Unless the water was high due to flooding, fish found it difficult to go farther upstream during spawning season and were thus 'trapped.' The hottest action to catch the big yellowcats roaming the Trap came in May when they spawned. The Old Dam, as it was locally called, the actual remants of the Alexander Dam built from 1908-11, sat at the head of the trap and was demolished just prior to the completion of Max Starcke Dam in 1951. Note the fishermen lining the banks and the wooden "community" boats everyone was free to use. This site was accessed through what is today Los Escondidos Drive. *Photo by Alexander Mills, courtesy of LCRA Archives.*

Johnnie Thompson (right) and a fishing buddy, standing on the corner near the old Marble Falls Messenger office, showing off fish caught on the Colorado River below Marble Falls. *Photo courtesy of Gloria Wagner.*

Far right: Ira Kennedy and J. Morton Burnham showing off their fish on Main Street Marble Falls, circa early 1900s. *Photo courtesy of Jody Bible.*

Virge Baugh (L) and Don Bridges Sr. with a mess of catfish in front of the original Blue Bonnet Cafe on Main Street. *Photo courtesy of Doug and Joy Michel.*

Tip Clark and John Maynard with a morning catch on the Colorado River at Marble Falls around 1908. *Photo courtesy of Madolyn Frasier.*

Far left: Jake Becker (L) and Klemons (Butch) Szymanski hold a good yellowcat in the early 1950s. *Photo courtesy Tommy Bailey.*

William Wimberly holds a hefty pair of big cats caught around 1948. *Photo courtesy of D.R. Jackson.*

Monte Tomerlin, George Lee, Ken Flory, John T. (Sonny) Taylor and Buddy Hamerick after fishing at The Ramp below Starcke Dam around 1957. The site below the dam became a hot spot for white bass when they spawned in late winter/early spring. *Photo courtesy of Sonny Taylor.*

Far left: Dale Robertson holds a good cat caught on a trotline in the early 1980s on Lake LBJ near Sportsmans' Lodge. *Photo courtesy of Dale Robertson.*

Odessa Wimberly Gibson admires these three big cats caught in May, 1948, by Budd and Wilbur Wimberly. *Photo courtesy of Donald Ray Jackson.*

Sonny Taylor won a set of new tires from Chester Barnett's Chevrolet dealership for catching this big yellowcat in 1952. *Photo courtesy of John F. Taylor.*

Junior Wimberly (left) works hard to heft this big yellowcat for a photo in 1969. Wilbur Wimberly shows off two more big cats from 1969. *Photos courtesy of Donald Ray Jackson.*

The Call of the Wild

On a hunt near Lampasas in 1952, J. Morton Burnham had a banner day calling up foxes. Accompanied by outdoor writer Hart Stilwell, who wanted to develop a story for True Magazine, Morton had a great day calling and the resultant story and photo by Stilwell literally started the calling business. By 1954 Winston and Murry were in business, working out of the home built by Capt. Jesse Burnham (their great grandfather) and opened Burnham Brothers in Marble Falls in 1959. *Photo by Hart Stilwell, courtesy Winston Burnham.*

Paul Ussery, Gene Ussery, Sam Ussery and Fritz Guenter with their dogs Red (famous for going to water with coons) and Brewster. Circa 1920s. *Photo courtesy of Lee Ussery.*

Murry and Winston Burnham opened Burnham Brothers Sporting Goods store at 212 Avenue H in 1959. In this 1959 photo they show off bobcats they called up in the local area with the short range call their father, J. Morton Burnham invented, and which the brothers modified and refined. The call was to make the two world famous in hunting circles. Their slogan was: "The critters come when called." The window to the left was later converted to hold rattlesnakes, which grabbed everyone's attention that came by the place. Great deer heads and other animals lined the upper walls of the store. The stuffed head of the 88.5-pound yellowcat (8.5 inches between the eyes) caught at Pedernales Falls by Bill Reimers and Don Casey was on display for many years. When archery became hot in the mid-sixties, Fred Bear would visit. For outdoor enthusiasts it became a mecca, a must-see place. Winston retired in 1982. Murry sold the buisness in 1992 and it was moved to Menard, still under the Burnham Brothers name. *Photo courtesy Winston Burnham.*

A. W. McLaughlin (left) digs through his tackle box, which he kept filled with his fine homemade lures, hunting for a lure for Winston Burnham at the Burnham ranch in South Texas. Mac, as everyone called him, was a well-known outdoors writer and photographer. Together with his buddy, Russell Tinsley, the two were acknowledged authorities on Texas fishing and hunting. Mac was also the master bass fisherman on Lake Marble Falls, always seen in his canoe quietly working the lower lake. For many years he was the outdoor writer and columnist for The Highlander. *Photo courtesy of Winston Burnham.*

In 1961 Roy Rogers called Murry and Winston Burnham and invited them to Los Angeles to visit his ranch and do some callin'. They called up this bobcat that Rogers is holding. For Murry (L) and Winston, this was one of their first big hunts outside of Texas and led to hunts Africa, Mexico and Canada. *Photo courtesy Winston Burnham.*

Don Cude (L) and John Taylor show off rattlesnakes killed at a den near the mouth of Sandy Creek (by modern day Sandy Harbor) in the early '30s. *Photo courtesy of Doug and Joy Michel.*

P.A. Walsh (1), Claud Shipp (2), E.J. Walsh (3), J.W. Hunnicutt (4), C.A. Reed (5), Lonnie McKean (6) and Don Bridges (7) show off a successful deer hunt. *Photo from Elizabeth Alexander Collection, courtesy Betty O'Connor.*

Johnnie Thompson, circa 1937. *Photo courtesy of Gloria Wagner.*

A Pictorial History of the Highland Lakes Area

Sports

Marble Falls championship girls basketball team, 1919, on the steps of the old granite school in their gold middies and purple bloomers. The team beat Burnet here 63-9, then beat them again in Burnet two weeks later 30-11. Addie Samford's colorful written account in 1919 states, "From that day on Burnet swore never to play us again." Marble Falls found it hard to get another game — their reputation preceded them — but finally played Live Oak in Bertram on a Friday evening and beat them 23-10. The drive to Bertram was slowed by muddy conditions. John Askew drove the team and six fans, all in one truck, from Bertram without lights. They stopped in Burnet to get the lights fixed, but they soon went out again. Manuevering in the dark, the truck kept getting stuck in the mud, and finally wound up at the O'Donnells near Fairland around 1 a.m. The tired team and its fans were rescued and arrived home around 3 a.m. The team included: (from top, L-R) Valree Bible Nanney (center), Clara Bell (goal tosser), Addie Samford Crawford (guard), Thelma Johnson Lobos (guard), Ruby Jones Miller (running center) and Nina (goal tosser). *Photo courtesy Nita Crawford Renick.*

Addie Samford (Crawford) models the Marble Falls girls basketball uniform in 1920, which includes gold middies and purple bloomers. *Photo courtesy Nita Crawford Renick.*

1938 Marble Falls Mustangs; the last team to attend high school in the old granite building. Front row (L-R): Darrell Dunaway, Joe Fry, J. B. Cox, Coach Kara Newton, Worth Green, J. C. Ramsdell, Thomas Lacy. Second row: Truman Wagenfuhr, Ralph Powell, Ray Wagenfuhr, Joe Castaneda, Johnny Mezger. Back row: Herman Wagenfuhr, C.F. Wall, John Frasier, Eugene Shirey Powell, Vernon Farmer. *Photo courtesy of Doug and Joy Michel.*

The 1939 Mustangs, 7-0-2, won Marble Falls' first district championship; tied Holland 13-13 in bi-district, with the Hornets advancing on first downs. First team in new senior high school, where they posed at the main entrance. Front row(L-R): Powell, Henry Michel, Sam Faubion, Wayne Waldrop, Leroy Phinney. Second row: unknown, Ray Wagenfuhr, Worth Green, Bobby Mezger, Buddy Crownover, unknown. Third row: Gaston Heffington, Herman Wagenfuhr, Bert Thompson, Gene Shirey Powell, Joe Castenada, JC McClish, Johnny Mezger, with Coach Kara Newton at the back. *Photo courtesy of Doug and Joy Michel.*

1942 Marble Falls Mustangs, regional champs, 8-0-0 overall, with a six game regular season due to WWII. First year Coach Frank Hefner's Mustangs scored 242 points and allowed none. Beat Center Point 58-0 in bi-district, then whipped Leander 26-0 to win the school's first regional championship. One of the great teams in Marble Falls football history, unscored upon in 1942 and the streak continued until the last game of 1943 — 16 games altogether, including two 0-0 ties against Round Rock and Florence in 1943. A&M Consolidated beat the district champion 1943 Mustangs in bi-district 27-0 to snap the string. Front row (L-R): William Herrington, Carol Nanney, Donald Crawford, Lyman Shaffer, George Wagenfuhr, Sonny Taylor, Henry (Ticks) Michel. Second row (L-R): Robert Whitman, Billy Mauldin, Wayne Riddell, Sam Faubion, Wayne Waldrop, Bill Smith, Deward Edwards, Clarence Phinney, Coach Frank Hefner. Third row: #6 Unknown, Malcolm Fluitt, Leroy Phinney, Jimmy Mezger, Harold Kennedy, Robert Lee Ebeling, Truman Wagenfuhr, Clayton Nolen. *Photo courtesy of Doug and Joy Michel.*

1942 Marble Falls Mustangs, bi-district champs, first team lineup, in front of the then new high school building. Coached by Frank Hefner, down linemen (L-R) are: Harold Kennedy, Malcolm Fluitt, Wayne Waldrop, Henry (Ticks) Michel, Robert Whitman, Wayne Riddell, Jimmy Mezger. Backs are: Clarence Phinney, Leroy Phinney, Sam Faubion, Bill Smith. *Photo courtesy of Doug and Joy Michel.*

1944 Marble Falls Mustangs, bi-district champs. Front (L-R): Managers Joy Green and Carlyle Wall. Second row, kneeling: Tate Gunn, Junior Burton, Clayton Nolen, Jack Guenter, Sonny Taylor, George Wagenfuhr, Willie Matern, Kenneth Proffitt, Doug Michel, Coach Frank Hefner. Third row: Buddy Lusinger, Richard Adams, #12 unknown, Bobby Becker, Rudolph Wagenfuhr, #18 unknown, Truman Wagenfuhr, Joe Wenmohs, Max Haile. Back row: Henry Wall, William Herrington, Jimmy Mezger, Robert Lee Ebeling, Richard Pigott, Clayton Mezger, Billy Hoskins. *Photo courtesy of Doug and Joy Michel.*

1944 Marble Falls Mustangs, bi-district champs, 9-1, 204-52. This team lost its opening game to Llano, 12-6. They won eight straight to win district championship, then beat A&M Consolidated 19-12 for bi-district before some 1,500 fans in Marble Falls, thought to be the largest crowd ever to attend a football game up to that time. This was the first string lineup. Linemen (L-R): William Herrington, Robert Lee Ebeling, Junior Burton, Clayton Nolen, Tate Gunn, George Wagenfuhr, Jimmy Mezger. Backfield: Joe Wenmohs, Jack Guenter, Sonny Taylor and (not visible except for legs) quarterback Willie Matern. *Photo courtesy of Doug and Joy Michel.*

The 1955-56 Regional champion Mustangs, 12-0, that started 'The Streak' of 26 consecutive wins. Front row: Manager Tommy Shifflett, Billy Naumann, Darrell Bible, Jimmy Taylor, Larry Lewis, Lyndon Rippy, Kenneth Smarr and Doyle Naumann. Second row: Curtis Karl, DeWayne Faith, Sam Debo, John Gregg, James Clark, Leecil Bowman, Bob Lewis, Kenneth Williams and Coach Bill Hammett. Third row: Coach Fritz Lehnhoff, Glenn Riddell, Joe Coats, Don Holland, Joe Herrington, Allen Edge, Norman Williamson, August Herrington, David Birch and Morris Clark. Back row: Daniel Vasquez, Myron Weir, Tommy Warren, Stanley Wyatt, Don Williamson, Dudley Grumbles and Ronald Sayers. *Photo courtesy of Madolyn Frasier.*

The 1956-57 Regional champion Mustangs, 12-0, that carried the streak to 25 games. Back row: Coach Lehnhoff, Tommy Shifflett (manager), Butch Sayers, Doyle Naumann, Don Holland, Lesuell Bowles, August Herrington, Sam Debo, Joe Herrington, Tommy Warren, Joe Coats, Myron Wier and Lloyd Clark. Middle row: John Gregg, DeWayne Faith, Wendell Thomas, Darrell Bible, Billy Naumann, Jim Taylor, Pepper Lewis, Bob Lewis, David Birch and Ralph Clark. Front row: Dan Vasquez, Gail New, Bill McMillian, Willis Lewis, Errol Sylvester, Dwight Denniston, Harvey Holland, Ray Coe, Lyndon Rippy and Royce Meador. *Photo courtesy of Madolyn Frasier.*

At the 1979 UIL State Meet, Carolyn Amos completed a tremendous track career by winning four gold medals in the long jump, triple jump, 100 and 200 dashes. She was the first woman ever to accomplish that historic achievement and gave Marble Falls second place in Class 2A. Amos tallied 25 points as a freshmen at the state meet 1976, was a member of the record-setting 440 relays in 1977 and 1978, and altogether scored some 120 points at the state meet in four years. *Photo courtesy of Novella Amos.*

(L-R) Sandra Abney, Carolyn Amos, anchor Barbara Conely, Sonya Clark and Coach Charline Bullion shown after they broke the Class AA State Meet record in the 440 relay in winning a gold medal with a time of 48.7 seconds. The next year these girls would not only break their own record with a time of 47.9 second but would also win the State Track and Field Championship in Class 2A, Marble Falls's first in track. *Photo courtesy of Bessie Jackson.*

Tamara Coburn traveled to the UIL State Meet all four of her years at Marble Falls, competing in 13 events (100-m, 200-m dashed, 400-m run, long and triple jumps) and winning nine medals, including 4 bronse, 4 silver and a gold medal in the long jump (19' 1.75") her senior year in 1993. *Photo courtesy of Jay and Betty Jo Becker Coburn.*

The 1992 Mustangs (13-1-1) advanced to the Class 3A semifinal round, farther than any Marble Falls team, where they lost to Cold Springs 32-29 in the Astrodome. *Photo courtesy of David Denney.*

Marble Falls defeated Abilene Wylie with a score of 43-39 at Brownwood, Texas. John Wilson, Melvin Armagost, Tony Haverda and Brian Smith. *Photo courtesy of Bessie Jackson.*

Marble Falls native David R. Birch became an accomplished boxer, compiling a 40-4 amateur record and winning regional Golden Gloves championships as a middleweight. Late in his career he turned pro, earning a 17-4 record with 13 knock outs. Shown in this early 1960s photo, he was a gifted puncher who knocked out opponents with either hand throughout this 57-8 career. *Photo courtesy of Jody Bible.*

Pitcher Terry Becker (top) and catcher Steve Roper pose before a 1967 Mustang game. Marble Falls didn't start baseball until 1961. These two were a part of the 1965 team which won the Mustangs' first district championship. *Photo courtesy of Ona Lou Roper.*

In 1957 Charley Taylor (center) came up with the idea of having an annual rodeo. He enlisted the help of his buddies Jack Rogers (left) and Bobby Burnam. They created the Marble Falls Rodeo Association and in 1958 produced the first rodeo, complete with a parade, street dance and rodeo queen (Arlene Bruns Rhoades). The MFRA soon added a junior rodeo and both events have become permanent fixtures in the summer. The rodeo was first held at the arena the MFRA built where J.M. Huber is located today, next to the railroad tracks at Avenue N. A new arena was later built some two miles south of Marble Falls and is the present site of the rodeo. Taylor became the early president of MFRA. When he retired, Rogers, with the able help of his wife Shirley, led the organization and has held the reins for the last 25 years. *Photo courtesy of Shirley Rogers.*

The first Marble Falls Rodeo queen, Arlene Bruns Rhoades, 1958. *Photo courtesy of Arlene Rhoades.*

Billy Herbert, with his horse Dixie Brown, won the Best All-Around Cowboy at the Texas State High School Rodeo in 1997, and was a member of the National Rodeo Championship Texas Team. *Photo courtesy of Billy Becker and The Highlander.*

A Pictorial History of the Highland Lakes Area

The Modern Era

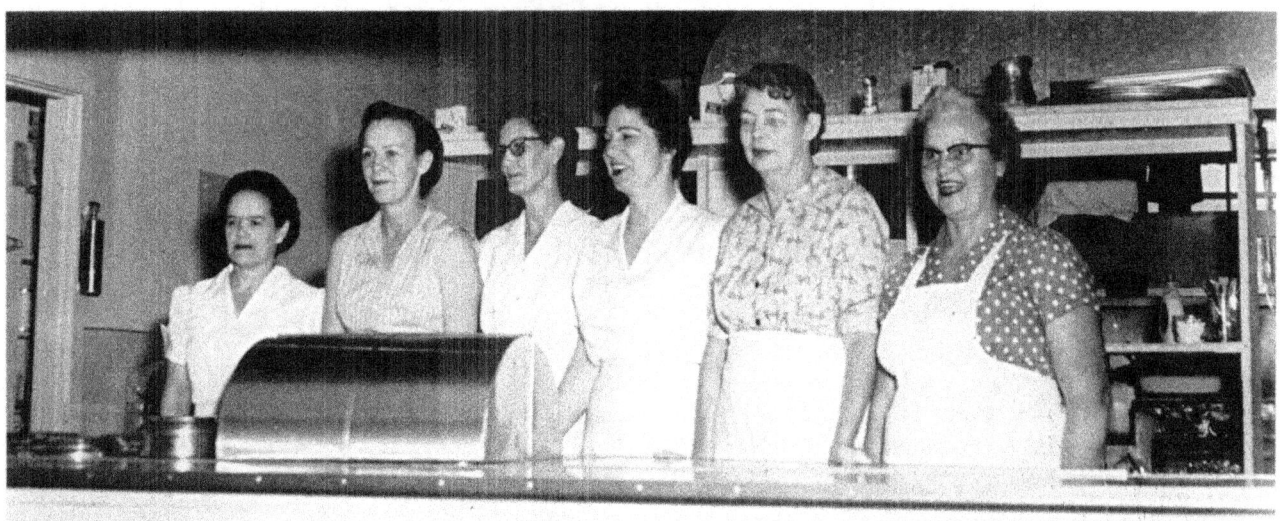

1960 Marble Falls school lunchroom cafeteria. Shown are: Martha Rippy, Ruth Forehand, Sarah Hardin, Leta Clayton, Alva Ealey and Beulah Heffington. *Photo courtesy of Shirley Rogers.*

Roger Gibson, Rose Gibson, Mary Gibson and Jane Gibson at the Gibson home in Marble Falls. *Photo courtesy of Rose Metzer.*

Central Texas ranching, farming and hunting was dramatically changed in 1964 when the Screwworm Eradication Program proved a great success. In the beginning, the program was privately funded and Ralph Ebeling Sr. headed the effort in this region to raise money and to promote the program. When it proved that it could eradicate screwworms with sterile flies, the state took over the program and to this day monitors importation and any infestation cases. In this photo from 1964, Ralph Jr., Marilyn, Ed, Ralph Sr. and Judith Ebeling hold boxes from the very first airborne sterile fly drop. *Photo courtesy of Annie Dee Hyatt Ebeling.*

Annie Louise Hohenberger Harton stands in front of the Hohenberger home in January, 1950. The house, some six and one-half miles south of Marble Falls on Hwy. 281, was constructed from stones gathered all across the southwestern United States. *Photo courtesy of Annie Harton.*

H.T. Ellison and grandson Russ Roper at the Ellison home in Marble Falls, circa 1952. *Photo courtesy of Ona Lou Roper.*

Mary Burnam with Tom Taylor, oldest child of Sonny and Norma Taylor, at the Burnam homestead in November, 1952. Founded by Capt. Jessie Burnam in the 1850s, this is one of the oldest continuous ranches in the region. The home later burned, the fourth time that has happened at the site, and was rebuilt. Bobby and Bertie Burnam now live there. Bobby and his brother Sam still work the ranch. The barn in the background, one of the oldest structures in the area, still remains in use to this day. *Photo courtesy of Sonny and Norma Taylor.*

Hiway Food and Ice grocery store on Hwy. 281 next to the Masonic building in December, 1952. Shown are: Oscar Bailey, Kenneth Brummett, Johnny and son Tommy Bailey. *Photo courtesy Tommy Bailey.*

Dock and Mary Belvin celebrated their 50th wedding anniversary in October, 1953, with (L-R) Lena Bailey, Mary Blankenship, Jim Belvin and Bertie Thompson. *Photo courtesy of Tommy Bailey.*

Ocie Goldman, Mrs. Ira Kennedy, Mr. Ira Kennedy, Opal Birch (Kennedy), Inez Bergen, Essie Wilson and Alma Lewis, June 19, 1954. *Photo courtesy of Jody Bible.*

The four Kennedy grandsons as teenagers in the 1950s at the Kennedy home on Pecan Valley Drive. They are (from L-R): Larry Goldman, David Birch, Freddy Goldman and Ernest Terry. *Photo courtesy of Jody Bible.*

John and Minnie Ramsdells 50th wedding anniversary in front of their home with all their children and grandchildren, circa 1955. *Photo courtesy of Myrtle Townsend.*

Clyde Griffin relaxes amid smoking furniture on the Nunnally and Griffin float in the first Rodeo Parade in 1958 as it passes in front of the Roper Hotel (then the Francis House Hotel). Their first attempt at a motto, "Relax — You're Fixed" might have unpleasant and comical connotations in a ranching community, it was pointed out, so just before the parade the motto was changed to "Relax — You're Insured" and survives to this day. The business became Nunnally Griffin & Dockery and exists today as NGD. *Photo courtesy of Clyde Griffin.*

The very first Confirmation class of Holy Cross Lutheran Church. Front row (L-R): Dawn Dilworth, Annie Hohenberger Harton and Dorne Michel. Back Row: Herman Wendler, Henry Hohenberger, two young men from Burnet and Pastor Goerdell. *Photo courtesy of Annie Harton.*

In 1978 St. Frederick's Baptist Church moved to its modern home at Avenue N and First Street. The church, organized in the home of Mrs. Dicie Yett in 1893, moved into the lower floor of the Blazing Star Lodge. In 1899 the congregation moved to South First Street and Avenue L, where it was called 'the church in the hollow'. In 1955, the church moved to Avenue N and First Street. St. Frederick's made its final move to the corner of Avenue N and Third Street in 1978. *Photo courtesy of St. Frederick's Baptist Church.*

During the 1980s Mr. Roy Martin worked for MH-MR and was a substitute teacher for Marble Falls ISD. He fashioned the African-American Achievers Program at St. Frederick's Baptist Church to teach about black figures in American history. *Photo courtesy of St. Frederick's Baptist Church.*

Pastor Reginald Brown with his wife, Linda Brown. Pastor Brown took over leadership of St. Frederick's Baptist Church in 1995, continuing over 100 years of service to the community. *Photo courtesy of St. Frederick's Baptist Church.*

Mr. Earl Moore, circa 1962. He became the eyes of the best friend he has ever known, General Johnson. Mr. Moore was brought to Texas at the age of three and his family was sold to Dr. Yett. During those years of the remarkable Johnson career, the General was aided faithfully by Moore. *Photo courtesy of St. Frederick's Baptist Church.*

Ms. Bessie Jackson was presented the Lone Star Council of Girl Scouts First Annual Women of Distinction Award and the Heb David Ashworth Award for contribution to the community and schoolboard as an excellent example of citizenship. *Photo courtesy of St. Frederick's Baptist Church.*

Gus and Lillian Michel at the 1976 Chamber of Commerce Banquet where Gloomy Gus received the 'Citizen of the Year' award. *Photo courtesy of Doug and Joy Michel.*

Chamber President Ron Mitchel of Horseshoe Bay presents Janella Pimpleton with the Marble Falls/Lake LBJ Chamber of Commerce's Outstanding Citizen Award. Pimpleton was also presented the Lifetime Achievement Award. She was recognized for her outstanding work at The Helping Center and St. Frederick's Baptist Church. Janella and her husband Herbert raised three children in Marble Falls. *Photo courtesy of St. Frederick's Baptist Church.*

Everyone turned out for the 100th anniversary of the old granite school building, still used today as the administrative headquarter of MFISD. Emcee Sonny Taylor speaks to the crowd. On the dais are: (L-R) John Kemper (Bluebonne Cafe), Bro. Max Copeland (First Baptist Church), unknown, Rev. Murray Johnson, Ron Mitchell (Horseshoe Bay), Mildred Galyean, Madolyn Frasier, Mayor Tony Hoague and School Board President Dale Bergman. *Photo courtesy of John F. (Sonny) Taylor.*

The Ford family, Christmas 1980. Front row: Ward Henry Ford and Helen Laree Ford. Back row: Vicky Lynn, David Lavern, Jerry Ward and Connie Laree. *Photo courtesy of D.R. Jackson.*

Children of Wanda Jackson, circa 1984. James Kenneth "Henry" Jackson, Travis Ira "Sonny" Jackson, Donald Ray Jackson, Myrtle Inez "Liz" Marx and Wanda Jean Walker. *Photo courtesy of D.R. Jackson.*

Jerry Michel reads the 100 years of history of Michel's to the gathered crowd on Main Street at the dedication of the Texas Historical Marker on May 18, 1991. *Photo courtesy of Doug and Joy Michel.*

On May 18, 1991, Michel's celebrated its 100-year-anniversary, complete with Texas Historic Designation marker. Observing the occasion were (L-R): Doug Michel, Sr., Doug Michel, Jr., Joy Michel, Diane Michel, with Doug and Diane's children Roxanne and Jackilyn. Doug Jr. is the fourth generation of Michel pharmacists to serve Marble Falls. *Photo courtesy of Doug and Joy Michel.*

One of the storied places in the area is Dead Man's Hole, some two miles south of Marble Falls. In the photo, Katie (left) and Wynona Becker peer into the mouth of the well-like cave in August, 1998. Ona Lou Roper and her family donated the mysterious landmark and surrounding acreage to Burnet County for a historical site. Walter Richter did extensive research and made the presentation to the Burnet County Historical Commission, which accepted the proposal and forwarded it to the state. The state soon designated Dead Man's Hole a Texas Historical Site. Burnet County completed the work to make the cave accessible to the public and it was dedicated in May, 1999. At the turn of the centrury, some 17 sets of bones were found in the cave that has had such a murderous history. Richter's great-grandfather, Judge Adolph Hoppe, was allegedly killed and thrown into the 155-foot deep hole. During the Civil War, Union sympathizers such as Noah Smithwick's friend, Capt. Hubbard, were killed and supposedly dumped in the cave. Because of such lurid tales, Dead Man's Hole has always been a mysterious part of the folklore of the area, seldom seen but always present. *Photo courtesy of Billy Becker.*

Hugh Reed organized the first community Christmas dinner on Christmas Day, 1994. With no sponsoring organization, Reed managed to find a place for the feast at a local restaurant, arrange the supplies and volunteers to cook, and is shown here serving the crowd which showed up. Reed, with the help of the community, has been able to continue the dinner every year since '94. *Photo courtesy of Clyde Griffin.*

This photo from Walter Richter is almost a twin to the cover photo of this volume provided by Joe Cude. They were both obviously shot from the same site by the same photographer in 1899. However, the Richter photo was printed in reverse (the negative was backwards when printed) and was not particulary recognizable. It is remarkable that each image has survived on its own for 100 years. *Photo courtesy of Robyn and Walter Richter.*

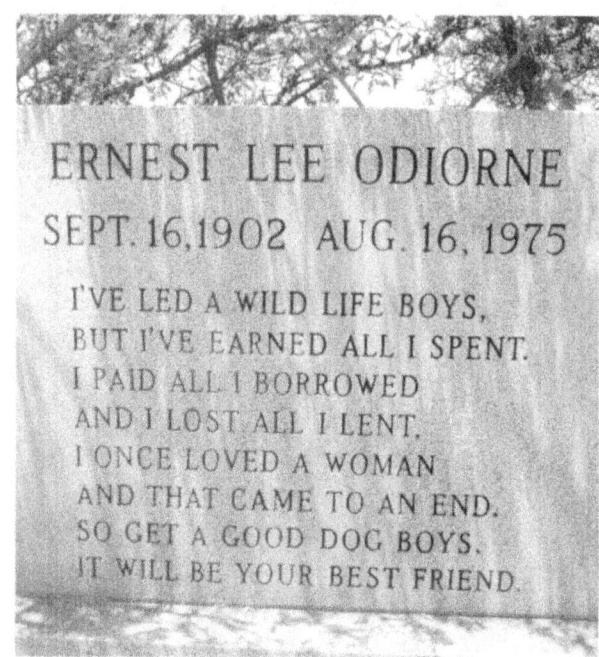

This is Lee Odiorne's tombstone in the Marble Falls Cemetery, with his final personal advice. Texas is famous for its collection of colorful characters, and Marble Falls is no exception. Sometimes these characters were people of great accomplishment, sometimes just rounders and story tellers who lived this life at full throttle, often creating more chaos than order. Some, like Lee, were an experience unto themselves. One night in 1966, Lee screeched into Trussell's Exxon, and jumped out, yelling, "Fill it up and put in two quarts of oil," as a woman laughed from the darkened interior of the old coupe. I filled the car with gas and checked the oil, which was about a quart and a half low. So, when Lee came back, I told him it wouldn't take two quarts, it would just blow out. "Hell, I don't care," he said with a big smile, "just put it in, and we'll see how far this old horse can run." I did, and he zoomed off down Hwy. 281 toward the river, blowing a trail of blue smoke into the hot summer night. Lee left a trail most everywhere he went, and like more than a few locals, he loved to see just how fast and far the horses could run. Only Lee would think of making people laugh in a cemetery, and in so doing, get the last laugh. It takes all kinds.

www.ingramcontent.com/pod-product-compliance
Lightning Source LLC
Chambersburg PA
CBHW060233240426
43671CB00016B/2934